THE *Fablehood* TRILOGY

THE *Fablehood* TRILOGY

What I Learned as a Child

John Manuel

City Bear Press
Manahawkin, New Jersey

Cover image
Cover and book design by Lynn Else

Copyright © 2023 by John Manuel

All rights reserved. No part of this publication may be reproduced, stored in a retrieval system, or transmitted in any form or by any means, electronic, mechanical, photocopying, recording, scanning, or otherwise, without either the prior written permission of the Publisher, City Bear Press.

Library of Congress Cataloging-in-Publication Data
[to come]
[last line CIP data]

ISBN: 978-0-692-1XXXX-X (paperback)
ISBN: 978-1-735XXXXX-X (e-book)

Published by City Bear Press
19 Henry Drive
Manahawkin, NJ 08050
www.citybearpress.com

Printed and bound in the
United States of America

*In memory of my beloved parents,
who have moved on to the kingdom of heaven.
Love always!*

Contents

Prologue ix
Acknowledgments xi
Introduction xiii
1. Yiayia Ephigenia 1
2. The Palette Man and His Last Supper 6
3. Cousin Comforting 9
4. Daydreamer 11
5. Hippy the Man 13
6. Connie, My Advocate Sister 17
7. Connie, the Peacemaker 21
8. My Beehive Keeper 25
9. My Brother, George 29
10. Glossa Adelphi 32
11. Uncle Dashing 34
12. Tinsel Tensions 39
13. Holiday Blues 43
14. Aunt Highball 46
15. Thanksgiving Surprise 51
16. Old Friends 56

THE Fablehood TRILOGY

17. Unexpected Cheesecake 63
18. Brotherly Angst 67
19. *Makrothimia* 73
20. Trips to Trips 76
21. Manuel's Comet 81
22. One Giant Leap 85
23. Puff the Magic Father 87
24. The Shop 93
25. Maternal Chairs 97
26. *Voltas* 104
27. Wallywood 107
28. The Asklepeion Mom 114
29. Follow the Bouncing Note 118
30. Kinder World 123
31. Recess Warfare 128
32. Bus Stop Buddies 131
33. Hangers On 134
34. Banana Splits 138
35. Faculty Faculties 142
36. Greek School Dropout 149
37. Button-Down Shirts 153
38. Altar Boy Antics 157
39. Bizarre Bazaar Boys 162
40. Outside the Sirtaki 167
41. The Late Great Fear of God 171
Epilogue 177

Prologue

The following stories, little vignettes, are offered from my own childhood—from two years old to when I was ten—and cover the people and places that taught me valuable life lessons. They are written as a gift to my children and grandchildren—a kind of periscope into a world they will never know, except by random photos and remembrances shared by myself and others. In writing these stories, I hope to preserve an image of days that were and are yet to come. Of course, these stories are told from the perspective of a child: some, will be humorous; others, not so. With hope, though, they will convey moments of appreciation for the people who influenced me and contributed to the person I am today. Perhaps you, too, will learn something about yourself in the process. To assist this process, I am providing my own moral or lesson with each story for your consideration. Please enjoy this mosaic of personalities!

Let me also say that my great inspiration for this endeavor comes from my long-time friend and bride, Karen. Others have asked me to write on several occasions, and I have kindly heard them, but have never started. With Karen's patience, her suggestive and

THE Fablehood TRILOGY

complementary approach, and her constant love and forgiveness, I discovered that I could not say no. And so now, as age is beginning its unwelcome advance, I am compelled, on behalf of my lovely bride, and in my mother's memory, to share these stories.

Acknowledgments

To Karen, my bride, for finding a way to get me writing and for motivating me along the journey. I am forever grateful to you!

To those, who read, proofread, edited, and made helpful suggestions to the manuscript. I am especially grateful to my daughter, Sarah Manuel Mandeville, my sister, Connie Manuel Gianulis, and my publisher, Andy McCabe, all of whom advised me with their thoughtful commentary.

Special recognition goes to Dr. Peter Kalellis, a priest, therapist, and prolific author, for helping me believe in myself.

For my children and grandchildren, for whom this is all written and for their prayers and support, and those who are the subjects of this manuscript. I love you all!

Introduction

BACKGROUND

Before I launch into all these memories, just a word about their background. The setting for these bite-sized stories is in the city of Lancaster, Pennsylvania, deep in the heartland of where you find Amish, Mennonite, and German American quilts. When my people, the Greeks from the island of Kos in the Eastern Aegean, moved here in the early decades of the twentieth century, they found work in mills, factories, fruit stands, and the like, but it was often not an easy mix with the locals. As was the custom with immigration, the new arrivals were not warmly embraced. If you stayed in your own ethnic neighborhood, you were tolerated, and so the Greeks had their own small ethnic enclave. It was in this world that my father, Steve Manuel, was born in Lancaster in 1931. Dad was the youngest of three children, the offspring of George and Ephigenia Manuel, both of whom were also immigrants from Kos.

My dad grew up in the 1950s, and was your typical James Dean rebel, jazzed out with a white t-shirt, with a pack of Camel non-filters rolled up in the short

THE Fablehood TRILOGY

sleeve. Wiry, highly strung, and lightly built, Dad was a revved up angry young man, hell bent to get back at the world. Quitting high school, but artistically talented, Dad enrolled in some art classes, but when his mother, my Yiayia, (Greek for grandmother), discovered that there were nude models used to inspire drawing, she quickly yanked him out of that sodomite place. Looking for love, Dad found a wife, an Irish American woman, Jerry, whom he soon married. In fact, Dad eloped on the very day that his brother, Tom, was getting married. His marital subterfuge eventually led to the birth of my half-brother, Steve, however, the nuptial bliss would not last longer than a year. Finding respite in divorce, Dad then enlisted in the U.S. Army, and began his life, unattached. Meanwhile, Yiayia would take matters of marriage for her son into her own hands.

Mom was born in 1932 (or 1931, according to a long-standing argument about birth dates between my mother and her older brother, Damianos), and also grew up on the idyllic island of Kos. During her formative teen years, the island was occupied successively by Italians, then Germans, until it was finally liberated in 1948. Among the middle children of six, born to John and Konstantavlinio Tripolitis, Mom was raised with the customs and traditions of her ancient Greek heritage. However, since Greece was at that time governed by Italy, she learned to speak, recite poetry, and sing songs in Italian, but spoke Greek at home. When the war broke out, and the Germans took a stranglehold on Hellas, she and the family had to survive under the most harrowing of circumstances. When liberation finally came, Mom, still just a teenager, could be seen in one of our treasured photographs, helping

Introduction

to lower the Union Jack, in preparation for raising the Greek flag to its rightful place.

With the tensions eased, the men and women of the island could go about freely and converse, and so it was during this time that Mom's fate was sealed by the force of tradition. Being the youngest girl of six children—four girls and two boys—when the time came for her to marry, there was no dowry left to offer to a potential suitor. As it was, after the "Great War," Mom worked as a secretary for an eminent doctor, for whom she had a romantic interest. However, before the love could be requited, Yiayia Ephigenia was poised to intervene on behalf of her wayward son, Steve.

The story goes that Mom's brother, Damianos, on behalf of Dad's Mom, showed Dad four photographs, each of a Greek woman from a well-respected family from Kos. He was asked to pick one of them, and his eyes fell on Mom, who was in the spring of her Mediterranean beauty. That was when Yiayia set up the *"proxenia,"* through my Uncle Damianos, the arrangement that would send Dad to Greece to meet Mom. Having no dowry to offer, Uncle Damianos offered a garnet ring to my father—that I have since inherited, and even given to my wife as a necklace. In reflecting on these times, my sweet mother would later say that although she had nothing material to offer her suitor, my father and her family would be content, because, as she often proclaimed, "America was my dowry."

Of course, the complication was that Mom was already in a wonderful relationship, and for her to marry someone she did not know would be to turn her back on love, and frankly, on the world she knew.

THE Fablehood TRILOGY

Her parents did not force her and gave her room to decide but feeling bound by duty to the family and to help them out financially, Mom agreed to the union. There was, by custom, about a month for them to get to know each other and to agree to the terms, but Mom had already decided that she would do what was most practical and best for her family. So, on June 10, 1954, at St. Nicholas church in the center of the town of Kos, Mom and Dad were married. Mom left her relationship behind and decided to move to America to fulfill her familial duty. In time, the fellow whom she loved would marry someone else and prosper in the reduced homeland of Greece. For Mom and Dad, however, the New World awaited them.

They would set up their home in Aberdeen, Maryland, where Dad was stationed at the Army Proving Grounds. Mom, who knew no English, found some solace at the Annunciation Church in Baltimore, where she offered her services as a babysitter. In one of the ironies of life, one of my parishioners, Tony Agapis, whom I knew while I was serving as a priest in Richmond, Virginia, was babysat by my mother during that period. In any event, when Dad's stint in the army was finished, they moved to Lancaster, Pennsylvania, our village and hometown.

One might think that the young couple would then set up shop and live happily ever after. Of course, that is not what happened in this tale. With his artistic gifts, Dad aimed to be a boat designer, a career that rapidly went nowhere since he did not work well in groups. He then went to barbering school and got a job with a group of barbers at the College Barber Shop by Franklin and Marshall College. Again, because he could not work with others,

Introduction

Dad went into business by himself. He set up shop on Sixth Street, a narrow side street on the west side of Lancaster, from where he would support his young family.

My parents moved into a traditional row home, with a front porch facing Southwest End Avenue. It was a well-built, solid-brick three-story home with plenty of room and access to great schools, neighborhoods, grocery stores, parks, and even the hospital. My earliest memories from this home are limited since I only lived there for a few brief years. Here's why.

Mom was busy raising children and keeping peace in the family. She needed a break and opportunity to reconnect with her roots. Having been away for some twelve years, she longed to return to Greece to visit her family and friends. So, in 1966, Mom had the good fortune to visit Greece. We were taken care of at the time by my Yiayia and my cousin, Ginny. While Mom was in Greece, during an age when folks could not easily get in touch with each other by phone, mail, or computer, Dad put his own plans into action. He found a long Cape Cod-style home on a couple of pristine acres at 1969 Millersville Pike, an address in the wealthier neighborhood. Without her knowledge or approval, Dad managed to put a down payment on a house that sold for $32,000, an enormous amount at that time. To purchase the house, Dad sold our existing house on Southwest End Avenue for a mere $17,000 to a crooked Greek realtor, who persuaded him to sell the house for the same amount that he had originally bought it. Hence, Dad was not able to reap any appreciation or profit from the move. Needless to say, when Mom came home

THE Fablehood TRILOGY

from her well-deserved trip, the home that she was living in here in America had already been sold. Here she was first a refugee from her precious homeland, and now a refugee from her newly adopted home.

Mom never went back to her home island again. She never again saw her mother or father or sisters or friends or family. Even though there would be many opportunities to return, many trips for her to jump on, and even a trip when Dad and my sister, Connie, visited in 1972, Mom never went back. Exiled, marooned, cheated, betrayed, or however one may color it, Mom was stung by Dad not once, but repeatedly. Sadly, regrettably, unfortunately, Dad turned out to be the master of the sneak purchase, a burdensome distinction that Mom never found easy to justify or accept. She stayed in Lancaster, adopting its culture and sights and customs and community as her new *chorio*, her village. Kos was gone forever; she would never see her home island again. Her *patrida* (beloved homeland) existed only in her fertile memory.

Mom accepted her fate to move to her new *patrida*, and to accept the distance of miles and years. She was content to stay where God had placed her, thinking that *ola einai grammena*, ("It is all written"), and that God had this move as his plan all along. She would not go back to Kos, not once, not ever. One painful departure was enough. Years later, when Mom was ill and widowed, and we had all grown up and moved away from Lancaster, my sister, Connie, offered to have Mom move to her residence in Williamsburg, Virginia. Connie would ask over and over again, with Mom always resisting as politely as she could. (She did not want to hurt Connie's good intentions and feelings.) Finally, she said, "I left my *patrida* (Kos) once already; I will not, and cannot, leave my new *patrida* (Lancaster); this is my homeland now." Connie—and all of us—would never press the question again.

And so, this is where I come from. The people and places that will be presented here form the village in which I was raised. Not everyone is recorded here, but certain individuals and circumstances, from which my personality and character have developed. Of course, as we all know, each and every one of us is the culmination of our environment and experiences. I hope that the good reader will be aware that I am respectful of every person who is mentioned here, and that I have only gratitude in my heart for their contributions to my life. I did not put them there, God did. And in so doing, the Lord has given me every opportunity to grow. I hope, then, that this work will be seen as an expression of deep thanksgiving for all those described. They have all made a lasting impression on me. Here, then, is my story offered for you, my gift to you, one vignette, one chip, at a time.

MY LIFE IN CHIPS

Welcome to my very own personal bag of "chips," short little passages pressed into this humble volume, to provide a full batch of crispy lessons. My good friend, Eric Goldman, does not remember this detail from our English classes in college, but when he wrote his papers, he would call them "chips," since they were so easy to read, and went down so easily. I owe him credit for this salty idea.

THE Fablehood TRILOGY

Few things are as addictive as the Utz potato chip. In fact, even referring to a mere single chip is a foolish mistake in judgment, for, as we all know too well, no one who loves chips ever stops at the very first one. Growing up in central Pennsylvania, in the idyllic City of Lancaster, I perfected the practice of chip gluttony, fisting not just one or two or three chips into my gaping mouth, but forming stacks and shoving them in, and even placing chips in Lebanon bologna sandwiches. As a matter of culinary curiosity, my brother, George, and I especially loved crushing the chips until they were mere crumb, before dousing them in ketchup every Saturday morning, while watching cartoons on TV.

SCHEMA

Yet more regarding chips.... These are attractive to me as a theme for this book because they are short and salty and frighteningly far too easy to consume. A good chip is also a work of art....Who could deny their beauty? The excellent Utz chip is sliced thinly from a cleaned and peeled raw potato, and then fried in clear vegetable oil until the chip is crisp, with just the slightest hint of golden-brown. They are then immediately dashed with salt—a whisper, not too much and not too little—until they are conveyed into puffed bags, sealed and delivered to your neighborhood grocer. They are not born from nature, but are crafted to be delightful, and if possible, enjoyed one at a time by folks who, by the way, never considered their health in the process. What the master creators of the Utz chip did have in mind, though, was the utter joy that can be derived from mere snacking. I am hoping, therefore, that the reader—my children and yours and anyone else with a self-indulgent appetite—will harbor a guiltless affection for the fragile yet delicious chip, arranged here as lessons from my experiences, delivered one little chip at a time, with hope and good salt, to fill a bag of days and years.

Regarding fables…. We are accustomed to thinking that the fable is a made-up story, like the homespun stories taught by a certain Aesop. But these are not made up or pretend scenarios. Everything that will be shared in this volume is as true as the air I am breathing. True, the experiences will most certainly be shaded by my colorations, but they reflect what a child saw and understood and absorbed at the time. If a negative experience is shared, it does not mean that the person or persons involved are resolutely bad nor that I am rendering some kind of personal deficiency. Rather, the fables, true as I can recall them, are presented to portray what really happened and what I truly felt at the time. I beg the reader for forgiveness if I ever cross the line into characterizations that may be less than flattering. To my mind and heart, these stories are true—well, as true as any child can recall. Enjoy the fables and the chips!

HOW TO DIGEST THESE CHIPS

As you know, I wrote this book for my family. *Fablehood* is primarily inspired and intended for my children and grandchildren, but also for anyone who

THE Fablehood TRILOGY

reads them. Here are some suggestions on how to consume these salty chips:

Nosh, Nosh, Nosh. Just enjoy these brief fables and the accompanying chips. After all, who doesn't enjoy a bag of chips occasionally. This variety is not so fattening, and with hope, may bring a smile to your face (or at least a grain of salt). Read them again and again alone or with another person, and as often as you like!

Breakfast musings. Eat a chip a day! If you are one of those folks who likes to begin their day with prayer, scripture, and meditation, then here is some food for thought. You may even consider reading one chapter a day during Lent or some other reflective time. (There are forty-plus chips.) Reflect over a cornflake or two. Most of all, enjoy!

Potluck meals. Since everyone loves a good discussion around the table, feel free to have a group reading of the book. These helpings are tastefully brief and easily consumable, so the group could simply read a chip or two and simply ask, "How was your meal?" Meaning: What are your thoughts? Can you identify with what was expressed here? How? The presenter could start with a lesson or just ask open-ended questions and see where the chips fall. (I couldn't resist!)

1
Yiayia Ephigenia

She had huge hands, immense, like catcher's mitts, tinged with a pungent scent of garlic and bleach. I knew this odor very well because those hands, those thick gloves of a grandmother were often near my nose and mouth. Her large, looming, and all-powerful presence, was inescapable, for this gargantuan "she" in this little vignette was my grandmother, in Greek, "Yiayia." The word, "Yiayia," is usually spun with golden reverence, but I cannot claim such cozy memories. I wish that I had felt affection toward her, but, in truth, I was terrified of Yiayia. Yiayia Ephigenia was my father's mother, the only grandparent I would ever meet, since my paternal grandfather had already died, and my mother's parents were firmly ensconced in a mythical and distant land, "the old country," Greece. So it was that Yiayia Ephigenia represented my one and only experience with the generational stratum of elders in my family. She was plenty to handle, and even more than I could possibly imagine.

    I recall one time when I was positioned snugly in the kitchen sink. Bath time was upon me, as one

THE Fablehood TRILOGY

of her hands held me tight to the cold metal bottom, pushing me flat to the surface like some fleshy suction cup, while the other hand, colossal and muscular, with thick gnarled fingers, cupped water and soap, impressing these upon my skin, flattening my nose with her paws, my eyes stinging from the soap. Occasionally, she would cover my mouth, so that my screams could not be heard. I felt powerless, like a rag doll, beaten, exhausted, and swept over by her immeasurable power. Yiayia was a force I could not forget, not at two or three, or ever. Even now, I can still feel her immense presence around me, her eyes, bulbous and magnified by thick coke-bottle glasses, her eyes bearing down upon me, to remind me that she could and would see everything. Escape was impossible. I went limp in her hands, and then felt the rough tossing and rolling, rubbing, and raking of my body under the towel. I could not wait to be dressed and off to bed, where my tears, at least, could soothe my crushed and humiliated flesh.

Then, another day would dawn, and back to the sink, this time to be wedged in to eat. Again, I was overcome by her power, though this time, with her one hand holding my mouth open by squeezing the back of my jaws, while the other hand shoveled soggy cornflakes into my gaping throat. I would scream, spit, bite, and do whatever I could to resist the onslaught of spoon after spoon of wilted cereal, while hearing her say, in shrill Greek, *"Fah-to! Fah-to!"* (Eat it! Eat it). These moments were anything but tender. Her voice would rise like the shrieking of a harpy eagle, her talons holding me fast, with the imminent threat of tearing me to pieces. *"Fah-to! Fah-to!"* (Eat it! Eat it!). Submit! Surrender! The scene could not have been more ridiculous! A haggard harridan force-feeding a defenseless two-year-old. I cannot believe I survived her onslaughts.

Of course, on the one hand, I suppose that the scene was funny and humorous in an exaggerated way. From this vantage point, this perspective of decades, when I say the words out loud now— *"Fah-to! Fah-to!"* —I can readily and easily laugh, as I hear the screechy shrillness of Yiayia's voice. Good stage material! But, on the other hand, this earliest memory in my life posed little humor for me at the time since I felt such utter terror at the prospect of being near her. Nevertheless, Yiayia fed, clothed, and bathed me, and, I suppose, in retrospect, she helped me survive, day after day, as a toddler, when my precious mother, or anyone else for that matter, was not around. Indeed, Mom was one of the few Greek mothers out there working, or rather, slaving away at the Slaymaker Lock Factory. But she did what she had to do. In any event, I suppose I should now be grateful. But the truth is that even to this day, I refuse to buy a box of Corn Flakes, or any other kind of cereal flakes, lest too much milk bring back a soggy experience of limp childhood recollections.

Furthermore, I should add, whenever these episodes occurred, I was at Aunt Esther's house, an old Victorian home, adorned with moth-balled sets of plastic-draped furniture, ancient lamps, and the brocaded curtains of an earlier, dustier era. I will say more about my aunt, Esther, later, but let it suffice for now that she was the constantly embittered sister of my father, the middle child of my Yiayia, and the mother of my cousin, Ginny. My aunt, Esther, and Yiayia, along with my cousin, Ginny, all lived in

THE Fablehood TRILOGY

this purloined home, and inside it, my Yiayia had her own room, a place that I felt forbidden to enter. It was not that I could not enter; I simply chose to avoid her room. I kept my distance, like any child who valued his life, because I knew all too well that the icons, which occupied a scarlet corner of her room, with their peering and traceable eyes, were Yiayia's personal agents, watching me, following me, waiting for me to fall. With their Byzantine stares, so unyielding and implacable, the eyes of the spooky saints would not leave me if, and when, I ever ventured into her room. And so I wisely kept my distance from those haunting eyes, those orbs that were so wickedly irradiated in fiery hues by a simple red votive light. Yiayia's room was certainly "off-limits" to me, a no-brainer to swiftly pass and avoid, lest the eyes of her iconic demons should follow me around and around again, and torture me with their penetrative stares.

Of course, Yiayia was just being her traditionally religious Greek Orthodox self, but what did I know or even care about that? All I knew was that Yiayia was scary, and that she was in touch with "the other world," one that I would happily prefer to avoid. No wonder I was so terrified of her! God forgive me, I know I sound awfully ungrateful, but when Yiayia died in 1970, when I was an impressionable eight years old, I must confess that I felt no pain or sorrow or sadness. All I could muster was relief, relief to the point of feeling that I could breathe again, relief, as if the wicked old witch had finally met her maker. O Lord, forgive me!

Nevertheless, I would like to finish this story with a better and more generous memory. Yiayia's grapevine presented an arbor of peace. For there

Yiayia Ephigenia

among the leaves and vines, I experienced one brief shining moment, where the sun shone brightly and I actually felt safe, if not downright proud, around Yiayia. The grapevine covered over and dominated a latticework structure behind her old brick house. Huge clusters of ripe grapes would descend from the wiry stems, in curly cues of heavy purples, mauves, and avocado-colored fertilities. The grapes were easily gathered by Yiayia, each cluster readily clutched within her sure hands. The perfectly formed symmetrical leaves would also be harvested, and I loved that they would be gathered in long skirt pockets, in old brown bags, in any box or bag that would receive them. Yiayia would plow through the grapevine as if she had created the grapes herself, as I suppose she did. After all, she certainly did not need any more attire than clunky black shoes, an apron, and hands large enough to hold sun-ripened clusters. No doubt about it: She was the master of the vineyard! Those moments remain my very best of Yiayia.

Terrifying, overwhelming, all-powerful, and seemingly ever-present, Yiayia was a force of nature. My first fable is broken, no, shattered in memory of her.

CHIP 1: *Never force; always encourage. In my life, I have rarely, if ever, responded well to motivation by force or coercion. I simply learned to dig in my heels from two years old. Consequently, I have rarely, if ever, motivated others, especially my own children, by compulsion, pressure, or force. Never force; always encourage.*

2

The Palette Man and His Last Supper

At my beloved sister Connie's home in Williamsburg, in her well-appointed dining room, with its colonial and tasteful decor, a large rectangular painting graces the wall. Depicted within an ornate frame, a well-designed portrait of the Last Supper is rendered in oil and mineral spirits. While I am obviously quite biased, I think our friend Mr. Da Vinci would approve of this imitation of his famous work. While his colors are muted and soft, more suggestive than declarative, this work calls out more intensely, as if the paints themselves could speak and lift their voices at the moment of being immortalized. The artist of this particular painting deliberately used colors, in perceptible texture, that were vibrant, swirling, and dramatic. Moreover, the artist depicted the faces of those seated around the table with so much expression that they appeared to be wide awake, and so keenly aware of the cup being offered to them that they could not be still, even in their stillness. They seemed to cry out from their oil-based world, raising their voices to proclaim that they were present at that most sacred moment. And, just to make sure we would take notice, one of the faces in the scene reflected not just some mythical personality, some random person, but rather, the face of the artist himself, my father, who depicted himself as one of the holy apostles. He is not set as one of the main characters, seated and formal in the center of the compositions, but is off to the side, half-standing, his whole body raised up in youthful anticipation, leaning forward over the table, with his hands set widely apart for support. His face is lifted upward, gazing, the whites of his eyes wide and inquisitive, searching for some understanding, some clue as to what possibly could be happening in this most sacred hour.

Whenever I see this work of true art, I always notice Dad in the brush strokes, and just like my father in the painting, I cannot help but become transfixed, having to edge closer, more and more, to grasp the gravity of what is being portrayed here. For here is a rendering of the Lord saying farewell at his final meal. It is veneration, worship of the immediate time, cast in oil paints and mineral spirits. I still gape with awe when I behold this picture, whether in person or in my mind's eye. This golden canvas is emblazoned upon my soul. Indeed, and without any exaggeration, I could easily describe every face around the table, especially the Lord's, with his eyes fixed toward heaven and his hands poised artfully over the bread and wine in blessing. In so many ways, this work could well be the masterpiece from my father's hand, and I am so deeply grateful that my lovely sister has preserved it so well. But I am blessed with yet another memory of this work of art.

I had to climb the long wooden stairwell to reach the third floor where my father's art studio was located. As I ascended, I was led more by my nose than by my stubby four-year-old legs, and that was due to the intoxicating fragrance of oil-based paints wafting around me. I rose up as far as the mineral spirits could take me, until I reached the doorway. Looking upward from my four-legged crawl, I could observe my dad bent over a slanted drafting table, over which a bendable light hung, while wafts of cigarette smoke curly-cued underneath, above, and beyond. A brush glistening with some dose of oil paint was in his right hand and a long pole in the other. Patches of paint could be discerned on his hands, t-shirt, and pants, while he was immersed amid creativity. While he was seated in a wooden slatted chair, one that could spin on its foundation, he whirled around toward me and looked directly at me. I can still remember the smile he gave me, and how he waved me to the top step and into his sacred studio. There, he invited me to look at what he was painting, the portrait of a certain member of the Last Supper.

CHIP 2: *Beauty is an eternal inspiration. In my life, I have always been blessed by what is beautiful and artful, and I thank my father for that gift. Hence, for me, everything I do, say, or think is measured by whether it is well-composed and beautiful. The on-going search for beauty captivates me and is my inspiration toward the eternal. Beauty is an eternal inspiration.*

3
Cousin Comforting

Let me say from the outset of this story, that I cannot remember a single detail of the whole thing. Whatever happened, I have to say, was beyond my personal control and has been shared with me by others. Though it will change nothing, I just want to say I am sorry. I am sorry for the horrid little brat that I was as a little child and apologize directly to my cousin, Ginny, thirteen years my senior, who was often burdened—and I mean severely burdened—to watch me as an infant and toddler. I owe her an immeasurable debt of gratitude.

My cousin, Ginny was the only daughter of my challenging Aunt Esther and, whenever my mother needed help, which was often, Ginny was called in. Ginny was bright and cheery and full of energy, and she deserved far better than she got from me. She did not realize that her abundant nurturing attentions would be tested to the limit by a most unagreeable boy. Even to use the term "boy" is a misnomer, for "animal" or "monster" would be more accurate terms to describe someone who would have been better in

THE Fablehood TRILOGY

a cage than anywhere else. I was what the Greeks, in their love for words, would call a *"thereeo,"* a wild and brutish and destructive Tasmanian Devil. My bratty behavior, which Ginny had to endure, was irrefutable evidence that I was not a pleasant or easy child. More creature than human, I would routinely and repeatedly climb out of my crib and fall to the floor. Then I would refuse to go to bed at all, preferring instead to shriek at the top of my lungs, until the tears and mucus would alter my appearance completely. I bit, scratched, and tortured Ginny, until I was finally physically strapped down in the bed to prevent me from moving. When I protested, she simply closed the bedroom door, and invited me to scream my way to sleep, which eventually, I did.

In today's overly medicated world, I would have been put on some kind of drug, like Ritalin. I am so grateful that I was not controlled by pills or any other artificial devices. Because of Ginny's saintly patience, I could holler and express myself to my heart's delight. Her sacrifice allowed me simply to be me, to have my own voice and eccentricities, even if I was regularly demonic and insane most of the time. Ginny endured, and I ensured. Ginny, if ever you read these words, I cannot thank you enough.

CHIP 3: *Never forget to say thanks. Some gifts in life can never actually be repaid. At such times, and with such folks, all you can do is say, "Thank you." This remembrance to be grateful is a graceful attitude of the heart, one that brings good perspective to the movement of life. In all things, both seen and unseen, Never forget to say thanks.*

4

Daydreamer

I was not always such a *"thereeo,"* a terror. There were many quiet times, silent times when I could suspend an entire universe in a shaft of light. I would lay flat on my back upon an oriental carpet in the living room and gaze upward into the sunlight pouring in from one of the windows. I would wave my arms and legs over the ornamental patterns beneath me, and sometimes I would trace them with my finger, and then wait until specks would float their way into the light. The dust would dance in the sunlight, spinning and whirling in arabesques, while I would reach up with my hand to swoosh the particles into a hundred destinations. Sometimes, I would focus on a single isolated speck from as far away as the ceiling, and I would strain to follow it across the airy universe of the room. My eyes would soon tire, and then I would shut them to rest, just a little, until I could return to my private reverie. I would also listen, as keenly as I could, just listen to hear if these little floating worlds could hear me or ever invite me over to play. But I was never allowed to settle and look

THE Fablehood TRILOGY

inside. I was on the outside, and perhaps they were too. Perhaps, I thought, there were other families on each of these tiny dots, little mothers and fathers, sisters and brothers, so I would deliberately look away, lest they be too embarrassed to be noticed. To keep myself hidden, I would also turn my body over, so that I was now lying face down toward the carpet. This way, I could run the hair of my head over the ornate floor, just enough to create some friction and some movement, and to give the falling specks some time to gather again. I certainly did not want to scare them. Then, I would turn back over again and agitate the floor and the air, so as to whisk the dust into the air to comfort me in my loneliness.

CHIP 4: *Imagination is the glider of the mind. A person is never truly alone, even when he is alone. Sometimes, perhaps most of the time, our best company is our own imagination. Our thoughts and our dreams can take us to incredible realms. With our imagination, we are never by ourselves. Imagination is the glider of the mind.*

5

Hippy the Man

Even from the perspective of a six-year-old, he was a beautiful man, a "man's man," an Adonis from the island of Rhodes. I would not have been surprised if he had arisen from the sea, like some masculine counterpart to the goddess Aphrodite. He struck a stunning pose, a figure like some living and breathing Hellenic statue. Tired of the merchant marine life, Hippocrates jumped ship and washed ashore somewhere in New York City, where he would reside for a while until he met my winsome cousin, Ginny. He was all bell-bottoms, Tom Jones grace, with European *futbol* athleticism in Adidas sneakers. Naturally, he had many Greek friends, with names like Taki and Mano, wearing burlap bags of cleats and soccer balls—the bare necessities of a bear of a man—rolling up in souped-up Torinos and Toronados. Many would end up calling him Pete, but my family affectionately called him "Hippy," short for Hippocrates (I mean, who wants to say that name all day), but he was anything but. Bell-bottoms and paisley shirts aside, Hippy was the guy you wanted next

THE Fablehood TRILOGY

to you in the foxhole. He was the guy who could talk sweetly to your mom or your aunt, with the smooth grace of island hospitality, but who you would want your sister to meet only if she had a couple of strong chaperones. He was the guy your mother could call on to fix the leak, mend the fence, or defend the home with nothing less than his bare hands. Hippy was a man for all men, and the desire, without a doubt in my mind, of many a woman. And my sweet cousin, Ginny, my patient and long-suffering babysitter, would soon fall head over heels for him.

Ginny had developed into one of those beautiful young women of the sixties, a woman who could stylize well in a mini-skirt and a bobbed haircut. Ginny had wide, expressive eyes, like milky almonds, set in a symmetrical classical Greek, oval-shaped face. When Ginny smiled or laughed, or "gave you her eyes," she could turn a head at every turn. I loved her grooviness, her "with-it" attitude, and her sass. I can still recall going to some restaurant on Columbia Avenue in Lancaster and watching Ginny hang out with her roller-skating boyfriend, doling out burgers and fries from car to car. Ginny had that Smokey Robinson and Diana Ross vibe, and so, when Ginny learned how to cut and dye hair, she was quite the item to reserve. And when Hippy discovered Ginny, well, who needed Sonny and Cher anymore?

Their wedding was at Brewer's Outlet in Lancaster. I know that does not sound so romantic, but it was one exceedingly far-out party! What a reception! All I can remember is how loud and crazy it was, and how much fun a little brat like myself could have, running in and out of Greek dance circles, and generally getting lost in the mayhem. Maybe it was

Hippy the Man

the first and only wedding I can recall from my years as a cub, but if that was what all weddings were like, then I was all in!

Eventually, the dust and confetti settled, and Ginny and Hippy got down to the business of homemaking, and children followed (more about them later). Hippy's entrance into the family was wonderful for all of us. With his smile and affection, Hippy made everyone feel special, especially an impressionable little rat like myself. Perhaps I myself needed such attention. Perhaps that is why I recall this one little memory from a tinseled Christmas during those velvet wall-papered times. We had the tradition of opening up our presents on Christmas Eve, at least for a while, and I remember getting a game that required more than one person to play. The game involved players, who would use little paddles to propel a ball to score a goal from one side of a playing surface to the other, sort of like a mini hockey arena, or dare I say it, a soccer field. I sat alone waiting for someone to come and play. Descending with grace and a Greek accent was Hippy, who happily, and might I add, competitively played with me. He did not "just let me win," to make me feel good; he competed, vied, went toe to toe with me—at least that is the way it seemed to me and how I prefer to remember it—and I loved every second of it! Eventually, I got tired, and when he got up for something or other, I fell asleep on the floor. Next thing I recall was Hippy picking me up and putting me to bed. I must have been half awake to even recall such a thing, but even from that age, I could recognize the striking combination of power and gentleness that Hippy possessed. I felt honored and deeply secure, and, as I drifted off to

THE Fablehood TRILOGY

sleep, I knew that I would recall this moment for the rest of my life. And so I have! Thank you, Hippy!

CHIP 5: *Love has powerful arms. Love carries us, always, even when we are unaware or completely blind of its immense power. No matter our age or situation, no matter how strong or independent we may feel, no matter what our conditions may be, we all need and hunger for love, affection, and attention. And sometimes, by the grace of God, we receive it, even when we do not know it is there, but once known, it is never forgotten. Love has powerful arms.*

6

Connie, My Advocate Sister

I have never had trouble believing in guardian angels, and that is because I have had one all my life. I even know her name, which is variously listed as Conitsa, Constance, Konstantavlinio, our maternal Yiayia's unusual name (oddly enough, named after a Byzantine princess for some reason). But I have always known my older sister by the name, "Connie," the appellation I am sure she prefers. Connie was very often my advocate, someone who could and would intervene in my life. With her overarching love and wisdom, she is, and always has been, someone I have been blessed with in my life; an angel who has always watched over me. I have been so deeply blessed in this way, that I am convinced that everyone should have such a guardian angel, a Connie in their lives. Thank God for her continuing wisdom. I am immensely blessed.

Connie, seven years my senior, had a wide latitude as the oldest among three siblings—George

THE Fablehood TRILOGY

being the middle child—and was a great boon for my mother and a wonder to behold. Because my mother was an immigrant and my dad was molded in the blue-collar world, Connie, as the oldest and savviest of us all, was our interpreter, our interactor, our interface with the outside world. If a letter had to be written to the teacher or the nurse or the principal, Connie was the author; if someone had to talk or intervene with others from the bank or the insurance agency, Connie was the mediator; if someone needed to make an order from a store or contest a bill, Connie was the attorney. She was our mother's go-between, her interlocutor, her ambassador and representative. And for me, she carried authority and wisdom in a language I could understand.

Hence, Connie was my bridge to all cultures, both our Hellenic heritage, with all its duties and obligations, and the fascinating world of the wild, rebellious American culture around us. I was never quite sure where I fitted in, since the hyphen between Greek and American was more like a cloud than a clear connective link. But at least Connie would know better, she would know how to navigate both worlds because she was hip, cool, affiliated on both ends of our cultural bridge. She could rattle off Greek, cook the food, and understand the demands of family, while also being the one who bought LP records, listened to the radio, knew which groups were in and which were out, who was the cool candidate, and what this whole Vietnam War was about. She was my cultural Athena of Lancaster, able to bridge the gossip of the Greek-speaking world, while also managing a firm grip with the word on the street. Admiration does not fully describe what I thought and felt

Connie, My Advocate Sister

about my sister. I adored her, and I would have gone to the ends of the earth to defend or protect her. Connie was akin to my mother, only far more accessible.

I loved her room as well. For such an obedient and smart girl, she had all the elements of teen rebellion, or perhaps the pulse of her age, displayed shamelessly on her walls. Musical acts like Jimmy Hendrix, Santana, Don McClean, Janis Ian, Three Dog Night, Crosby, Stills, Nash, & Young, Chicago 1, 2, 3, 4, an so on… and many other popular vox artifacts that could be uncovered in her coolest of rooms. I remember feeling oddly amused, aroused, and ashamed, all at the same time, while studiously examining a cover of a Santana album, which featured a completely naked black woman in a comely reclined position. I did not know anything about sex, except being oddly aware that this album cover was very sexy and that my eyes should avert it, but could not. My sister was the "good girl," and yet, she possessed such forbidden contraband in her room. What boy my age would not be intrigued by the fruit of all this stimulation? Besides, she introduced me to a new world of music, particularly a little band known as the Beatles.

If it weren't for Connie, I would never have heard of them, except that one night she uncovered one of the secrets for me. We were laying side by side together on her bed. (Many times I would lay close to her and just touch her hair softly, which she enjoyed.) On this occasion, she turned to me and declared in the most somber voice I had ever heard her speak, proclaiming, "The age is over, the era is done, the 60s are coming to an end, and some are even saying that the Beatles may be breaking up soon. They even say, 'Paul is dead.'" "Oh my," I thought, "Who

THE Fablehood TRILOGY

is Paul? And how come I don't know him?" I knew the Beatles were a group, and I knew "Hey Jude" and "Ob-La-Di, Ob-La-Da," but now my all-knowing sister was announcing that something serious or some mysterious guy named Paul was dying. Sometime after that heavy pronouncement, sometime late in the evening, some moment at some darkened hour of the night, a new song, a final song, was featured on my sister's nightstand radio. The song was entitled, "The Long and Winding Road," and as it played its mournful tune, I knew, I felt, I empathized with my all-knowing sister. An era was indeed coming to an end.

CHIP 6: *Listen twice; advance once. Listen carefully to the words of someone who has gone before you. They are wise for a reason. God provides each of us with advocates and advisors all along the way of life. Heed them. Listen twice; advance once.*

7

Connie, the Peacemaker

Because of her placement as the firstborn among the three of us children, Connie had duties and prerogatives that George and I simply did not possess. Expectations were completely different for us, as Connie always seemed to be under a different set of rules from us (Hmm!). She was watched more than us, even followed and pursued by our mother, as if something horrible was going to happen. Poor Connie chafed under this persistent and distrustful supervision, but she never complained, not at least to me.

Well, okay, maybe she did complain, but privately to her gaggle of leggy pubescent friends. Her whole "girl world" was a wonder to me. They were so different, smelled better, and even moved differently. I wanted to study them further, as they were quite the curiosity to me. But they always seemed to move in "feminine wave," the tug of which I was not allowed to enter. They sat and talked close together, as if guarding the spaces between them, making sure that prying little eyes and ears (such as I had) would

THE Fablehood TRILOGY

look no further. And then there was the whispering—lots and lots of whispering and giggles that were baffling to me. I had no idea what they were saying, and they were clearly not going to tell me. And, when they were not cupping their hands by their ears, they had transistor radios near them instead. They were a corps of sisters that included—as far as I can recall—Cindy, Janie, and Maria—and they formed an impenetrable sorority, and I was the dork who hung around them for some reason. Behind their hair, so neatly set behind lightly colored headbands, their pastel mod chinos, and slip-on shoes, these young ladies had their own group style and secret language. They chuckled knowingly among themselves, as they enjoyed the "inside joke" and the hidden gossipy gems. They were Connie's pals and, even then, I knew that they were her outlet from the pressures of our home, or more specifically, from the expectations of our mom. Mom watched over Connie, and it was clear that, even though we were all special to her, there was a special relationship with Connie, and rightly so.

But alas, I have neglected to describe this guardian angel. Willowy and thin, with long brown hair and vibrant chestnut-colored eyes, Connie moved with the grace of a Mary Tyler Moore. Smart, observant, quick, and socially adept, Connie was lightyears ahead of George and me in maturity. She was the child our mom could put forward as proof that there was intelligent life in our home. We all lumbered about, our knuckles clearly dragging on the floor, while she seemed to run at a faster and more efficient pace. No wonder, then, that our mother entrusted Connie with more responsibility and authority than we could ever

Connie, the Peacemaker

muster. It was her duty to keep the house clean and make sure that we did our share of duties to keep it that way. More than once, my "beloved sister" would grab me by the ear and twist it, until I submitted to do some chore that she wanted done. I was terrified that she might get really angry and pummel me, but, after a while, all she needed to do was simply stare at me, and I got the message very quickly. I hated her toughness, but I understood what was going on. She was our mother's little captain. Connie did the bidding of the general, and that was the way the law was written. So, I accepted it, albeit begrudgingly.

But then came more serious and difficult times, when Connie's deputy role for our mother would transform into a defensive role against our father. Dad would often get severely drunk, usually on a case of beer, and when he did, he would become extremely loud and bellicose. His language would be peppered with the ugliest and foulest of words, directed exclusively at our poor mother. He would say the most insane and disrespectful things, too indecent for me to even dignify on paper. This insanity would go on night after night, with the real fear that physical abuse might follow the verbal. All three of us children were terrified for our mother's safety, since dad's anger was volatile in ways that we could not imagine. His rages would depress us and leave us feeling shell-shocked and bewildered. And the longer this pattern went on, the patience of my sister became thinner.

Until one day he went too far, and Connie had had enough. So, when he had launched into yet another of his vicious tirades, Connie stood up and said, "Don't you think you have said enough? Stop

THE Fablehood TRILOGY

already. We have all had enough of your drunken behavior!" I could not believe my ears. Our mother was in shock, and George and I wondered if Connie would survive. But my dad got up, cast some insults in the direction of mother and daughter, again, calling them names unfit to print, and stormed off. But the Rubicon was crossed, and our mother was never alone again.

CHIP 7: *Truth always prevails. And this is so because truth is far stronger than fear. Even though fear can intimidate, paralyze, and devastate one's forward journey. Unopposed, evil wins. But the proclamation of truth, conveyed by courage, never fails. Where truth is insisted upon, lovingly, gently, inexorably, it always triumphs. Truth always prevails.*

8

My Beehive Keeper

If you combine cigarette smoke with a cloud of hair spray, you will realize that my Aunt Esther had just passed by. If you wanted to find her, then just follow the conical beehive hairdo, wait a second for a smart-aleck remark, listen for the clink and jangle of some jewelry, and then pick up the scent of some overpowering perfume, and you will have found her. She was the middle child of my father's siblings—Uncle Tom was the eldest, then Aunt Esther, and finally my dad, Steve—and she was the poster child of the difficulties and inferiorities related to her unlucky placement. She developed, therefore, a personality that demanded attention and refused to be ignored. Aunt Esther was a tour de force, an individual who rarely, if ever, withheld her opinion on anyone or anything. It did not matter who you were, your age, social stature, or what your business, Aunt Esther was always direct. She loved gossip of any kind and the more salacious, the better. In retrospect, she simply voiced what others were thinking, but she did this without restraint or filter (except for her cigarettes). With

THE Fablehood TRILOGY

her hairstyle stuck somewhere in 1949, and her furs and baubles to match, my irrepressible aunt could, and often would, launch into a rant, salted with such language that it would cause even a Navy Seabee to blush. I will leave the details of such a monologue to the reader's imagination.

Nevertheless, she could be as sweet and tender as a butterfly, at least to me, her "favorite nephew." I knew, even as a child, that all Aunt Esther really wanted was attention, perhaps too much so, but I was certain that loneliness was the cause of her suffering. Respect, kindness, gentleness, and consideration were her inner needs, but these were often loudly implored by harsh outward demands. For instance, whenever someone went to Arlan's—the nearest department store—she would always ask the person when they had returned whether they had bought her something. That something could be anything from chocolate nonpareils to popcorn, and even jewelry. She would often lament if she was not included on some little trip, and especially the big trips, for example, to the beach. And when she eventually did accompany her clan, Aunt Esther would insist on going to the most expensive seafood place the beach town of Wildwood could offer. Even now, when I am at the Jersey Shore and drive by Urey's Seafood, I think of her champagne tastes. Yet, despite all these seemingly selfish and irrational requests or demands, I perceived a vulnerable person, who just wanted love. Her needs were really interior, but she could not express them, so they came out in the most vulgar and material forms.

I think she sensed my own tenderness toward her, so I became her little whipping boy. For instance,

My Beehive Keeper

if we were watching TV or just "yakking" in the same room together, Aunt Esther would whine that her corns were hurting her. I had no idea what a "corn" was, until she unfurled her gnarled knotty feet and revealed them to me. My job, at first requested, and later expected, was to rub her corns, which I most dutifully did. Unpleasant, to say the least, I performed my duty out of respect, and perhaps, from some small fear of her anger. In any event, she would coo with pleasure and lean her head back, as if I were some long-lost lover. It was the least I could do.

When she made another request, which was always inevitable, would I mind going to the local mini-market ("Turkey Hill"), and get her some Pall Mall Longs? With one of the cigarettes balanced upon her lip, and even before I could respond, she had the cash ready, and sent me on my way. And so I would go, at just seven or eight years old. When I approached the counter, the guy there would already know what to pull down off the back shelf. I gave him the required funds then return with my dirty inappropriate banned goods, and she would smile contentedly. And so would I!

Over the years, Aunt Esther and I would learn to sit down and talk, and whenever she would rant and rave, I would employ the art of ignorance until she was done. When I became a young adult, Aunt Esther would liberally and casually quip—with a smile on her lips and a teasing wink— "Good God, what happened to you! You must have gained weight. You look like hell!" (Thanks, Aunt Esther). She would laugh and light up a cigarette in honor of her own devilish impropriety. In gratitude for my toleration, my respect, and I suppose my ministrations to her

THE Fablehood TRILOGY

oft-ailing corns, my aunt would make me a bowl of skordalia, a dish consisting of garlic, soft bread or potato, olive oil, vinegar, lemon, and garlic and more garlic. It was eaten as a spread on a cracker, or some bread, and would leave you unable to speak to anyone in public for days. But it was delicious, and she would often make me this dish as her expression of love. Later in life, at the reception following my first ordination to the holy diaconate, she made sure that skordalia was on the menu. I am still grateful for her loving gesture, and for the clove of garlic and vinegar that she was.

CHIP 8: *Never judge a lemon by its peel. There is more pulp to the fruit than meets the eyes. So it is with people; and so, never judge a sourpuss by the sour. Maybe they just want to be noticed and appreciated. A little love goes a long way to sweetening the sour. Never judge a lemon by its peel.*

9

My Brother, George

You would have to see his hands to believe me when I say that they are exquisitely beautiful. While my hands, and in particular my fingers, are short and stubby, my brother George's hands are graced with long, nimble, elegant fingers. When he opens his hand across a keyboard, an octave is easily covered by the breadth of his reach. I am not exaggerating when I say that his hands are probably the most beautiful that I have ever seen. George could have used his hand for Michelangelo's *David*, and still his would be superior. His refined fingers could grasp any object, anything from a fishing fly to a hammer, and the effort would come across with pristine elegance. Beautiful hands!

And, powerful as well. George possessed a manly strength that my DNA simply passed by on me. He could lift, carry, build, join, lift again, carry, and so forth far more than I could ever muster. In every category, George was physically superior, and he also possessed a mechanically oriented mind. As my dad would say, and was a hundred percent correct, "George is good with his hands."

That was so true, and so also was my jealousy. I am ashamed to admit it, but I spent years looking at George with an attitude that was so unfair and selfish. But confound it, he actually could do anything with his hands. I recall him playing the piano and being able to master the keys with such ease and appreciate all kinds of classical music. I seethed with admiration. And then he would produce something out of wood in my dad's shop, something beautiful, something extraordinary. He would use a lathe, a router, a table saw, a skill saw, a belt sander, and various other tools that I hadn't the foggiest idea how to operate. Moreover, he did it skillfully and masterfully and then move on to something else, like photography, gardening, tennis, and so on. He was a whirl of tremendous God-given talent, and I could not contain my ugly attitude. I found myself hoping that he would not do well, or just not as well as he was doing, or just fail. My spirit was mean, hideous, even monstrous. The jealousy consumed me.

My mother, perceiving this disgusting pallor in my soul, brought it to my attention, which, of course, I denied. But deep inside, I knew she was right, and that I would need to change the course of my inner voice, lest I poison myself completely. By exposing my feelings, she was able to denude them of their power and hold over me. By the plain power of my mother's insight, I could see a newer, broader way, a more generous way, whose perspective was wider than my own self-insisting viewpoint. She pointed out for me that each of us has gifts in our own fields, as God has willed, so that it happened that George

My Brother, George

was strong in areas where I was not, and I was strong where he was not. In her inimitable maternal wisdom, she revealed that we are each wired differently, a fundamental reality, and that itself is a worthy blessing, and not a place of contention. She urged us both to allow nothing to come between us, and thank God, even over the course of all these decades, nothing has.

As an addendum, my Aunt Esther, would also take great license to comment on our "brotherly love." She noticed the two of us brothers, in tension, and sometimes fighting. I asked her what she thought about our constant bickering, and she answered, "Oh, you'll be alright. The fact that you two are fighting, and can continue to fight, is a way of showing how close you both are to each other. Now, if you could not fight, why then, that would be a real problem, because you would not be close enough to care. So, don't worry. Trust me. I know about fighting. You two are fine!" And so we were and continue to be.

CHIP 9: *Each of us has our own distinctive fingerprint. No two are ever alike. God has a blessing for each of us, and each of us is called to give back that blessing to God. This act of returning the gift to the Great Giver is the stuff of life and the incense of God's glorification. There is no jealousy or strife, then, when we recall that every one of us is one-of-a-kind and once-for-all-time. We are all designed to fulfill life with our gifts and give God the glory. Each of us has our own distinctive fingerprint.*

10
Glossa Adelphi

Whenever I hear the song, "Daniel," by Sir Elton John, I am taken back to when I first heard it, back to the darkness of when my brother George and I shared a bedroom. In the rich darkness, with both of us staring wistfully at the basement ceiling, in the pitch quiet of the night, we would raise our senses to see anything that cracked or moved. When we weren't listening to the radio or to some tape, we would hear the walls creaking and the coughing noises of the heater clicking on and off. As we lay flat on our backs, staring pensively into the enveloping darkness, we could be heard whispering messages, exchanging dreams, and occasionally even disagreeing, which would lead to terrible tensions, fights, and blow ups. Thankfully, we were able to settle most of our differences, and this was, I discovered, because we spoke a common language.

Today, of course, no one would understand our brotherly dialect, but we took a certain private pride in speaking in our own distinct way. The patter, starting with a high note, and descending to a lower one

Glossa Adelphi

with each succession of verses of it, went something like this: "Banga, a linga, a junga, a singa; (lower) banga, a linga. a junga, a singa; (lower still) banga, a linga, a junga, a singa." We would sing this rhythmically and repeatedly until we both got tired of it and fell asleep. What did it mean? I have no idea, but it was comforting to say these words together, to have a way of communicating all our own. Love creates its own lingua. The truth is that we both treasured those quiet moments, and I am sure that, if I said our magical phrase today, even at the risk of embarrassment or over exposure, George would be listening, just as he always has!

CHIP 10: *The tongue is the rudder of Love. How it moves changes the world one syllable and breath at a time. When it is withheld or misdirected, it wounds. But when properly steered the tongue directs the journey of life. A word well-intended can change the navigator's arc. So it is that Love, on any level, creates its own language. This common language, even between rival brothers, keeps us together, even when we are pulling apart. The tongue is the rudder of Love.*

11

Uncle Dashing

Swooping curves accentuate the strokes of the royal blue "M" poised at the front entrance of my home. Stylized in a magnified italic font, the iron letter was created by a man as graceful as the arc in the initial itself. With a flair for the dramatic, the emblematic "M" remained for decades on my parents' house, until I retrieved it upon my mother's passing and hung it upon my own home. But this adornment was not just a representation of our Manuel family, it was also a statement of the man who designed and created it in the first place. That man made an immense impression upon me.

    He was our Gene Kelly, smooth and charismatic; he was our Arnold Palmer, athletic on the fairway, the green, and in the cup; he was our Gary Cooper, our Cary Grant, our Jimmy Stewart, returning triumphantly from the great war; a dashing and gallant figure; he was my Uncle Tom. He was the oldest and most accomplished of the three Manuel children, the eldest child of Papou George and Yiayia Ephigenia. He was the ex-ship gunner, the golfer, the athlete,

Uncle Dashing

with the well-chiseled physique, the jawline, the dimple, the charming squinting smile, the polo shirt master, the one who could build with his hands and teach others in a classroom, he was the hero whenever he arrived at our home in Lancaster. Uncle Tom cast a long shadow.

Whenever he visited from Philadelphia, where he worked as an industrial arts (shop) teacher, with his bride, Aunt Ann Jacobs, and their three ornery children, it was as if a light had been turned on, where formerly all was dark and drab. He brought energy and joy into the house, and it was obvious, even to a little kid like me, that whoever met my Uncle Tom was enthralled by him. He was the "golden boy" that men admired, and whom women admired even more. He was the cool, dashing uncle, who could show you how to handle a golf club and land a ball anywhere you wanted. He could show you how to play a game, how to cook on the grill, how to do anything you wanted. He was our "Uncle Dashing," so cool and so lively that you just had to be around him.

I can vividly recall how Uncle Tom would come every year around Thanksgiving, and after the meal, take out cord after cord of Christmas lights to adorn our lengthy, handsome Cape Cod style home. Evergreens in the front yard would shine with large bulbed lights—blues and whites, greens and reds—and the whole house would soon take on the celebratory plumage of Christmas. Indeed, it was as if he initiated the great holiday for us, as if the feast of Christmas could not, and would not occur, without Uncle Tom's faithful and delightful decorations.

A word on "decorations," which may seem shallow or merely cosmetic, but, in this case, I would say

THE Fablehood TRILOGY

these adornments were essential. They brought meaning to what was left bare and unidentified. Here, also, was a man who saw a darkened and drab and depressing home, where the opposite should have been true. So, he took it upon himself to set our home ablaze with vivid lights, a welcome contrast from its former state. Uncle Tom brought us, if even briefly on the outside, a new sense of ourselves, a breath of fresh air, a new light, a bridge to a better and healthier place—whatever metaphor is employed—the effect was the same. We went from darkness to light. Every bulb made an illuminating difference. To this day, when I go outside to decorate my own front yard, I think of Uncle Tom with gratitude. I can see what motivated him—a love for beauty and the creation of it for all to see and behold. With Uncle Tom, there was no haphazard, indifferent tossing of lights on trees. No, here now was an artist at work, one who cared about awakening us to love the holiday with all its luminescence. He changed Christmas for us, and for that I am forever grateful.

No wonder I adored him and vowed, even at the age of six, that I wanted to be just like him. Moreover, I thought, if I ever had a son, I would name him after this stellar man, after whom, of course, my son Thomas is named. For not only was he the grand hero of the Manuel family, he even deigned to play with a little kid like me. I was starstruck!

And then, the unthinkable happened. This man of steel would need a heart bypass, a procedure not available in 1969. (The surgery only began to be practiced in 1970.) After a very rapid decline, Uncle Tom died at the age of 44. The funeral was held the very next day, according to Jewish custom, but at the

Uncle Dashing

Orthodox Church. The shock of his passing led us all to a depression so abysmal that my parents neglected to decorate outside for Christmas, as Uncle Tom did, until Karen and I returned the custom, some fifteen years later. My cousins, Dougie, Michael, and Kathy would need counseling and therapy for years, and my Aunt Ann was never the same afterward. Worst of all, my Yiayia Ephigenia was so shattered, so devastated, that she passed away from a broken heart just a year later. For myself, my uncle's tragic passing was my first real encounter with death. I have rarely mourned as emotionally and totally as I did then. His death effectively shut down the lights of my childhood. In my heart, I knew that I would remember him forever.

As an addendum to this story, sometime in my early teens, I became a boy scout, a decision I should never have made. I disdained the whole clannish, paramilitary atmosphere of the troops. It just wasn't any fun. I scarcely recall why I even joined in the first place, but the shameful reality was that my commitment was piss-poor. In any event, the reason I mention this brief episode in my youth is because, at some point, I was involved in a merit badge exhibition, and since I had nothing to share, I grabbed all of my uncle's trophies and medals, a great number of them, earned during his prolific athletic career, and I displayed them. By the end of the evening, however, every one of the items was gone, lost forever, picked up by grubby little hands, intent on grasping an artifact for selfish, personal glory. To my shame, and eternal regret, I had managed to lose all of my uncle's tributes and honors—and all for nothing. He and his legacy did not deserve such an undignified

THE Fablehood TRILOGY

demise. If you can hear me, Uncle Tom, I am still so very, very sorry.

CHIP 11: *A falling star never fails; it always inspires even in its descent. Occasionally, God sends us a shooting star, if for no other reason than to renew our belief in the heavens and in the wonder of it all. Uncle Tom may your memory be eternal. A falling star never fails; it always inspires even in its descent.*

12

Tinsel Tensions

Who knew that such a insignificant thing as tinsel could be so contentious? But indeed, it was. I mentioned that the Christmas decorating ceased when my Uncle Tom died and did not begin again until Karen and I were on the scene. However, the inside of the house, or to be more specific, the Christmas tree was still something we continued to adorn. But a simple thing can often become a most difficult task. Allow me to illustrate.

My dad would always be the one to go out and get the tree, and for a number of years, the trees were even live, that is, balled up and set to be planted in the yard after the Yule festivities. But as time passed, my sister, Connie, got involved in both tree selection and its dressing. My dad would look for the biggest tree that he could find and manage to haul; Connie thought of how it would fit in the house. Dad wanted a wide tree, something with a huge girth to fill up a whole room; Connie sought the svelte and symmetrical among the trees, something that would not get in the way of folks passing it. Dad liked the sharp needles and something Nordic; Connie loved the white pines, soft needles, and something we could all feel comfortable around. Tree selection would eventually become a contentious and prickly subject. And so, we ended up with some pretty unusual trees.

Then there was the lighting. Dad loved the large bulbs, and a garish array of colors, even blinking lights. Not so for Connie, who thought lights should be one uniform color, preferably white, and preferably small. They should be set deep in the tree, allowing the beauty of the hunter green flora to predominate. Dad just threw the lights on and was done in ten minutes; Connie worked painstakingly to assure that the tree had balance.

Once the lights were set in place, the real tension would ensue—decorations. Dad, again, would just throw stuff on the tree with a sort of Jackson Pollack artistry and intensity. Not so Connie. The large bulbs, especially the reds and greens, would need to be placed deep within the tree, thus creating a harmonious background. This would leave the outer branches and twigs room to carry the weight of smaller and more personalized treats. Then there were the candy canes and garlands that had to be added. Dad followed suit by simply heaving them all over the arbor, creating a mistletoe madness. The garlands were thick boas and brocades that had the quality of dimestore costuming coupled with a velour chic reminiscent of the seventies. Yeah, Connie was not going to go for that! Dad's "correction" would need to be re-corrected and properly adorned sometime later.

The final indignity came in the form of little silvery metallic strips, commonly known as tinsel. With this material, Dad embraced his greatest joy. He

Tinsel Tensions

would hurl large clumps of the celluloid product on the unsuspecting tree, until it was literally draped, nay, drowned in the silver snowfall. Boxes and boxes of this chemical fire-hazard were tossed onto a dry tree, shimmering against the hot bulbs. We were one step away from permanent disaster. But Dad loved his decorations! I honestly think that Dad was going for an outdated Victorian effect, something overgrown, wild, and unkempt, something you would find in a musty old parlor in downtown Lancaster, some conglomeration that would have appealed to my Dad's origins in the thirties and forties. Who knows?!

One thing for sure was that for Connie, and I would venture to say for my Mom as well, the total picture was artless and vulgar, and that's being nice. When Dad left the room, or perhaps when he went to sleep—in any event, in his absence—the grand editing began. Connie would instruct George and me to take off all the tinsel and return it to their emptied boxes. In place of globs, she would meticulously articulate each strand of tinsel to key positions around the tree, so that it indeed started to resemble a trinket or bauble from yesteryear. The tinsels would descend from each limb with delicacy, as if held on by the merest adherence. Her attention to this work was most admirable, and the overall effect quite impressive, although I was petrified that Dad would walk in and discover our "improvement" to his mastery; thankfully, he never did. Indeed, I am sure he noticed the improvement and simply left it that way. The garlands were simplified, and some were replaced with cords and beads, and the thoughtful editing made the tree not simply presentable, but, I must say, artful and tasteful. Connie's rather persistent, indeed obsessive,

THE Fablehood TRILOGY

attitude with the tree also struck me as something admirable. She had a vision and stuck with it to the end. And to think that it simply came down to moving a little tinsel from here to there.

CHIP 12: *Less is more. If a Christmas tree needs pruning and benefits from trimming, then the same applies to persons. A little personal editing is a good, and necessary, thing. Less is more.*

13
Holiday Blues

One of the most important episodes in my youth was the bluish mood that descended upon our family at Christmas. Christmas and New Year were sources of terrible anxiety that offered us the potential of untold torment for one disdainful reason: alcohol. While commercials and advertisements would regularly extol its sparkling qualities, we experienced these spirits in quite the opposite light.

Dad always seemed to have a "drinking problem," but it would manifest itself as an angry ogre during the holidays. Every Christmas would have a cloud hanging over it, as if the sky was going to fall upon us. What would start off as a little time to exchange gifts would end up with him berating and bullying Mom and behaving like a child. It was as if he would deliberately seek ways to suck the life out of Christmas. While Mom would gift him with the usual socks and underwear, Dad would counter with an immense five or ten pound box of cheap chocolates, that he would have already eaten in his grotesque stupor. We all hated him for how he acted every Christmas Eve, and then be too hungover during Christmas to be of any reasonable company. Every year, Christmas was either dismantled by his antics or threatened with the possibility of his boorish behavior. To wit, Dad routinely ruined Christmas. I cannot recall when this reality started; it simply was always there.

Then there was that abominable "celebration" that morons across the globe called "New Year's Day," as everyday isn't itself a new day and the beginning of a new year. For our family this evening was even worse than Christmas, because Dad would insist on going to the church dance, originally with Mom, but then, by himself. While at this grand community social event, Dad would get quickly plastered, that is, if he was not already shit-faced. There, among all her friends and peers, Dad would put Mom down and disgrace her. She was mortified and terribly embarrassed, and this pattern would repeat itself year after year.

What's worse is that we could all see it coming. His holiday blues would follow Thanksgiving and wend their way through Christmas to the New Year celebration, wreaking destruction in its wake. He would become a gray version of himself, and that was during the day. At night, the cans of beer never stopped flowing, and the disaster followed from day to day and from year to year. For all of us, then, the holidays were anything but festive. Try as we might, pretend as we might, or even forgive as we might, we could never forget. How could we? The next bottle of blues was always just around the corner.

To this day, I need to fight off my own set of blues during the holidays. Christmas is thankfully recovered.

Holiday Blues

However, I avoid any large gathering at New Year's Eve, preferring instead to spend it quietly with family and friends. I have forgiven Dad; he could not help himself. But the scars and scabs are still there and trying to forget simply does not work well for me at this time of year.

CHIP 13: *No blue is bluer than the holiday blue. There is no surprise that "The Holidays" exacerbate tender wounds and brittle relationships, especially because folks are gathered so close together. In such circumstances, after the wounding, one can forgive an injury, and one must, but the debilitation in one's soul may last for years and years. There is a reason for the shades and hues. No blue is bluer than the holiday blue.*

14

Aunt Highball

If all things "New Yawk": bagels and lox, pastrami and corn beef, cheesecake, and thin crust pizza, could regularly be delivered to my childhood address, then my Aunt Ann Jacobs would be at the door. Associated with such a delivery would be a squawky package containing all the neurotic tensions and anxieties usually associated with "The Big Apple." And she would be my streetwise aunt, who, without any effort at all, oozed the culture of the well-known five-boroughs. And so it was that in our very Hellenic home, we enjoyed the occasional visitations of Uncle Tom's family, and in particular, his bride, Aunt Ann Jacobs. The reason I add the last name, which of course would properly be "Manuel," is because the Jacobs nomenclature emphasized her Jewish background. Whether this was her choice or not, I do not know, but the appellation, Ann Jacobs, became our regular lingua within the family. I do not know if anyone meant it as an antisemitic slur, since it would not have mattered who would have married my Uncle Tom; the women of our family were going

Aunt Highball

to be circumspect no matter what. From our perspective, though, we loved her as our aunt, and we enjoyed her particular Gotham eccentricities.

I would even go so far as to say that it was her cultural differences that made her so very appealing to us, at least to me. I noticed that, over the course of time, she and her menorah of culture was not so much different from ours. Though she had different holidays and rites of passage, we truly experienced a kinship that was comforting, familiar, and bonding as a family of ancient peoples, basically the same people, Jews and Greeks alike in brotherhood. We attended the bar mitzvahs and holy days of her tradition, and they attended the baptisms and feast days of our folks. We all got along wonderfully, and the three of us, Connie, George, and I found easy play partners in Dougie, Michael, and Kathy. I have no idea how the two of them met, but I am especially grateful that Uncle Tom and Aunt Ann were able to marry, albeit at a civil wedding, and not in the church, since such unions are simply not permitted in the Orthodox Church. Oy, I love saying that we have a Jewish side to our heritage.

Now, regarding Aunt Ann, she could usually be found with a long cigarette in one hand and a highball in the other. She especially liked gin and tonic, a spirt combination that would lead my mom to purchase Schweppes Tonic Water, Beefeater Gin, and limes, a concoction with which she was totally unfamiliar. Sometimes, when she was talking in her usual expressive Long Island drawl, the cigarette and the drink would share the same hand. Her ciggy's, by the way, were of the sophisticated metropolitan variety, a brand called Montclair. I suppose a simple Camel would not do here. There always seemed to be a puff of smoke near her mouth and eyes, as if she were constantly enshrouded, speaking behind a cloud of carcinogens. As she tawked, I always thought she was on the verge of choking or coughing, but then she would laugh in a crow-like honk, and her eyes would light up with the humor or slant of something that was being discussed, especially if she herself had brought it up. I do not know why, but whenever she tawked, her eyes seemed to always be half shut, and her voice on a constant rise in volume. Even as a snotty-nosed kid, I loved her drama and histrionics, which seemed to find unusual intensity whenever she talked about Uncle Tom and his work and obligations, or when she complained about the heavy burden that she alone had to bear in raising their erstwhile children. There always seemed to be some problem that she would squawk about, while my uncle smiled gently and remained quiet, and my mother listened intently and generously. I can still hear Aunt Ann say, "O Mitsa (my mom's nickname)," and then she would launch again into yet another tirade of issues that, even then, seemed more entertainment than actual issue.

    I enjoyed her immensely, and when Uncle Tom died, even I could witness how her whole world imploded. Of course, this was most understandable, but the reality was that after his death, nothing was ever the same between our families. We kept in touch, even when they all moved down to Florida to start a new life. But the intimacy, and the fun, carefree Camelot was gone forever. Over the years, we all sent Christmas and Hanukkah cards, and she loved that we were still connected. I felt such love and sweetness

Aunt Highball

from her, and when I married Karen, I was touched that she was happy for me. We continued to send her cards and to enjoy our link with her. How deeply saddened we were, when Karen and I learned that Aunt Ann had died. I was also crushed to learn of the passing of two of her children, Dougie and Michael. Dougie was a professional lifeguard at Miami Beach. Michael struggled with drug dependency and addiction all his life, even from the time we were children. I am not sure what caused their deaths, but I pray for God's mercy and their memory to be eternal. Thank God, our cousin Kathy is still alive and residing in Fort Lauderdale, and that we keep in touch.

As an addendum here on my cousins, we all got along like hellions recently liberated from prison. We had a ball playing like wild fiends together. My Dad and Uncle Tom both had BB and pellet guns, and we, of course, proceeded to have our shoot-outs in the basement of our home. We would also throw darts full force, or rather, as hard as we could, into the wood paneling in the basement, just to see who could get the dart stuck there. During Hurricane Agnes in 1972, or some other storm, we all went out and swam in the puddles, even though power lines were downed everywhere, and the streets were filled only with police cars and other emergency vehicles. There were also sharp pointy Jarts to toss about (and avoid), as well as wrestling until someone cried out, pillow fights, mattress thumping, mudpie making, and engaging in illicit tractor rides, to name just a few of the crazy and insane games we enjoyed and miraculously survived. I must admit that, although it was dangerous, it was also exhilarating, even for a four-eyed runt like myself. I still get a rush of adren-

THE Fablehood TRILOGY

aline, a shot of oxygen just thinking of those crazy times. We now rightfully mourn the passing of our libertine days with our gaggle of hooligan cousins. It was all such magical fun. When, as an adult, Connie and I went to the basement of our childhood home to make necessary assessments, we could still see the pellet and dart perforations in the thick pine paneling. Nostalgia certainly comes in strange forms!

But that all drifted away upon Uncle Tom's sad and tragic passing at forty-four years old. I admit that when I crossed that age threshold, I was a nervous, as if lightning might strike twice. That moment, of course, has passed.

But, in my memory, there is my sparky Aunt Ann, still smiling, and still enduring all the losses, the passing of her debonair husband, and the tragic demise of her two vivacious boys. There are no greater losses in this life, and I feel indebted to her for her example of handling them with such beauty and grace. I am all the better for having such a colorful and courageous person in my life.

CHIP 14: *An odd-shaped gem still casts a radiant glint. Love knows no borders or restraints but joins according to its one will, wherever and however and to whomever it wills. Love governs itself and hews to no one. Love is universal and invincible and ever beautiful, no matter who the subject may be. An odd-shaped gem still casts a radiant glint.*

15

Thanksgiving Surprise

Ah, Thanksgiving! That great American holiday, where even swarthy immigrant families, such as ours, can pause to give thanks for the blessings we have all received. Ah, yes, Thanksgiving! The supreme equalizer, where everyone's voice counts, where each member of the family can make his or her own contribution.

Good Lord, Thanksgiving! Thank God it comes only once a year!

Now, as a concept, a theory, an idea put into motion, this whole thing isn't bad. Why, it's even downright noble, that is, until it is actually pressed into service. As we all know, this most native of feast days is built upon gathering family around a table and offering up prayers of gratitude. Lovely ideas! There are, however, two major problems—if not many more—with this scenario. The first is the "gathering of family," the second is "the table."

First, *the gathering of family*. What a charming idea, if only it were guaranteed to work, and by that, I mean peacefully. Assembling my Yiayia, my aunts and

THE Fablehood TRILOGY

uncles, and all their children, my cousins, and their friends, plus the people I live with, well, that is akin to collecting all kinds of explosives and arranging them as close to a firepit as possible. Great idea! Getting all the relatives together—wonderful, thoughtful, unifying, preserving, and loving, all of it so good in theory, and yet, so disastrous in practice. The problem is not with the idea, which I have already gushed about, but rather, with the constituents, that is, the people in the family themselves. Honestly, if I were to have a party, and my intention was to have a good time and have everyone get along, well, I am pretty sure that not all of the folks in my family would be invited. The volatility of the whole situation stems, I think, from the naive attempt to get folks together, while conditions are simply not ideal; too much "relational tenderness." Hence, we invite our families to share a meal with delicacy and ideal intentions, which are so readily flustered when the histories of anguished relationships are not quite forgotten, or there is fundamentally bad chemistry between certain relatives, or when family members are too easily triggered because they are in the midst of personal trials and do not want to be disturbed. Put even a smidgeon of these details together, and the potential for disaster multiplies exponentially. Oh, and add that the gathering is one full of Greeks. Enough said!

Then, of course, there is *the table* full of the potluck items that have been contributed by family members. A meal together is ideally such a wonderful idea, but only in the realm of ideas. But in this environment, the individual fuses are particularly sensitive and may get lit at any moment. Thanksgiving is so often a potential powder keg because it

Thanksgiving Surprise

mixes ultra-sensitivities and skin-thin vulnerabilities with easy temptations of judgment and possible criticisms. Allow me to illustrate.

We were at Yiayia's house, which was filled with all our olive-complected relatives, who willfully and cooperatively participated in the potluck meal. The host generally prepares the turkey, or whatever the main course may be. Also attendant to the main course was the filling that would go into the bird. A lot of pressure rested upon getting these items just right. Prepare a dry turkey, for instance, and who knows what sparks may fly. Well, we were all at the long dining room table, you know, the one that is never used except for these kinds of occasions. Everyone was present, even my Uncle Tom's boxer dog, Champ, who loved sitting under the table. Aunt Esther, with help from Ginny and Yiayia, had prepared the turkey and the gravy, and that was wonderful. They also made pastitsio, rice pilaf, and coupled with the other items, the meal was mostly set. Except for the filling or stuffing.

"Filling," as a food concept, is really the reflection of one's culture and heritage. People take pride in their particular expression of filling and can sometimes be just a tad sensitive about it. There was the "American" filling, which featured bread and carrots and celery and such, and then there was the "Greek" filling. Greek filling was generally filled with hamburger, onions, spices, cinnamon, pine nuts, and even raisins, depending on the region. In this case, however, there was a rather different, though culturally authentic, item in the stuffing, for which I and most of the other children could not help but express our disdain. Anticipating something savory and delicious, we instead had the misfortune to bite into small pieces of liver that had been liberally interspersed throughout the stuffing. Responding with loud vocalized wretches did not endear us to most of the tolerant adults, but especially to Aunt Esther and to Yiayia, who were clearly not amused. We could be seen spitting out the offensive tarry meat. The offense had been received, and the fireworks ensued.

What followed was a screaming match between my fiery Aunt Esther and my dad over how horribly rude we were. Dad understood our position, though his mother and sister would have none of it. He championed our disdain for the food, and they did not appreciate his interference. Then the eruption occurred between them, and it was a free for all, while everyone else was wise enough to stay out of the fracas. Of course, on top of the whole food discussion, ancient family issues were dredged up, old hostilities, resentments, forgotten or misplaced appreciations, words said decades ago that should have stayed buried rather than brought up here. Add to these disagreements the presence of liquor, and soon the temperature became heated beyond control.

Here, then, was a "normal" Thanksgiving. Thank God, it comes only once a year!

The last I can recall was that I kept my head down for as long as I could and did not look up at all. My mom squeezed my hand under the table, the message of which I understood implicitly. From that point on, at our thanksgivings were multiple fillings and two renderings of the Greek edition. Thank God for small plates!

Thanksgiving Surprise

CHIP 15: *Family tables are full of all kinds of fruits and nuts. We cannot help if they are our loved ones and relatives. Pass the gravy and move on. And, to keep the peace, unless asked, keep your opinions to yourself. Family tables are full of all kinds of fruits and nuts.*

16

Old Friends

I was the only one to call him "Are-Us," instead of "Ahh-Ris," as was common. I was the only one who knew about "the Granny Wombat," "the weatherman," "the tent," and "play the ball." These were all words I would hear again and again, upon my visits to Aris's house, phrases that still resonate with me. I was the only one in our little realm to understand those terms, and yet, as it turned out, not to understand them at all. And so, allow me to describe the world and the person of my dear and closest friend.

We should all be blessed to call someone "my best friend." Aris was my best friend. We loved playing together, and we had much in common—both children of immigrant mothers, both from a similar Hellenic culture, and both with time enough to know each other well. Sporting sandals, with an olive complexion, and dark wavy hair, Aris had the look of the charming Mediterranean lad. He was the portrait of a boy accustomed to wind, water, and the Greek sun. Aris was fluent in both Greek and English, well-traveled, and seemed far older and more mature than his years. Separated by only a year (I was older), we did everything together. If he was not at my home, then I was at his. Curious, mischievous, and flush with adventure, we were like brothers, apt to play with a few sticks or some rocks or just with the time we had. We had a blissful friendship.

Sadly, though, as the years of our childhood waned, we began to have increasingly less in common. While we would play without boundaries or constraints, our actual relationship was not the carefree, easygoing lark that one might assume about the wonder years. Just the opposite. The son of my mother's dear friend, Georgina, Aris was very much a survivor and an adventurer. Even from that time, I could sense that our playing, our little games and imaginative scaffolding, were forms of escape. As time went by, I would understand why.

In the meantime, even as a child, I was aware that Aris was altogether different from other children. Most kids of that time played with balls and bats and bikes. Aris was not your typical rugrat, not in the least. For instance, he had a money collection with assorted paper and coin denominations that were all neatly and perfectly arrayed in appropriate books. Of their supposed value and provenance, Aris would articulate, with particular attention to notes, markings, and other such minutiae as to form an informed assessment. I never met anyone else his age who sounded more like a banker or a broker as a seven-year-old. Even at five and six and seven years old, I was bewildered to hear about all this meaningless observations. None of his stuff made sense to me. I just knew something was wrong, terribly wrong.

THE Fablehood TRILOGY

His toys were just as obsessively arranged as his money collection. I was astonished to see how orderly his cars were arranged, all in large boxes with neat compartments for each mini mobile or Hot Wheels. Everything had its place and was impeccably organized. I was lucky to have even one or two small cars to play with at my house, but here was an entire automobile plant in his third-floor closet. Add the tracking and electronic controls for the speedway, upon which the cars traveled, and you now had a sporting dream-world the envy of any rugged boy. There it was in all its glory, the grand racetrack, and we would race cars for hours. But when boredom eventually set in, we would personalize certain cars. We would give them names and personalities and race them off against each other. There was one car that we both noticed and soon identified as our own. It was an old white Model T vehicle, with a canopy and more squeaky wheels than the slick corvette or Porsche. But we both fell in love with this car, and we each claimed it for ourselves. We called "it" a "her," and her name was "the Granny Wombat," and whenever she raced, and whichever car she raced against, she always won handily. Granny kicked ass! We made sure of it. Even from the distance of all these years, I can still hear our unrestrained guffaws and laughter, as we celebrated her victories. And we both loved her intensely. But I could see that her victories meant so much more to Aris than to me. He truly reveled—even to the extent of changing his posture from sitting to crouching to standing, from apparent play to beaming pride—as she crossed the finish lines. I loved our little Granny Wombat, and I thought this was all just pretend, fun and games. So I thought.

Old Friends

Another arena of our play world was under a tent, or sometimes under blankets draped over some chairs. I recall one time, when we covered some bushes outside with some sheets, and our play began its usual advance. We played a game called "the Weatherman," where each of us got a chance to tell the forecast and to change the weather, and the other person had to act it out. So, for instance, I might say, "I'm the weatherman, and it's going to snow meatballs!" Then Aris would act out the falling of hamburger and sausage, stopping to eat some, and moving on to his turn. And this would go on and on, even with sound effects and props, with the tent acting as our own manageable world, the sky our will, and the walls our intentions. I remember, very well then, when Aris was acting out a storm, and the wind was "howling," as best as we could muster such sounds, and the walls were tumbling about, and he tumbled into me, and smiled. He smiled, wryly, coyly, as if he were hiding something and deliberately not saying it; his eyes sparkling and looking directly into mine, his body nestled near to mine, and his breath panting and heavy, and so he paused. He was way too close, I thought, which made me feel very uncomfortable. This was all just goofy play, and that's all it was going to be, that is, from my perspective. But at that moment, I noticed his wild-eyed hunger and intensity, as if I was in our humble tent with a tiger rather than a tyke, and so I cast out my arms and flipped off the whole assembly. The electricity of the moment was immediately defused, and I said that I did not want to play anymore. He was obviously very upset with me, and responded with anger, tossing the sheets and such, and walking away, seething. I remember walking around his backyard, meandering around, just trying to clear my mind. He had gone off to the garage, apparently to straighten something up, or whatever.

In the meantime, his mother, an elegant Greek woman with a taste for European haute couture style, noticed that we were distant and not talking to each other. She came out and called for him. With his eyes moist and reddened, Aris came out of the garage, and walked up to his mother. She could sense that something was wrong, and, in good Greek motherly fashion, offered us something to eat. I said yes, and he said no, and he did so in a most emphatic way. It was a firm no, an angry and dominant NO, and so food was clearly and resolutely off the table. Then she said words that are still burned into my brain, seared by sadness and pity, "Aristedes, play the ball!" We stood frozen. I could feel the embarrassment and anger welling up in my dear friend, as he stood still as a statue. She went over to the garage, found a ball, and, holding the ball out in front of her matronly apron, implored once more, "Aristedes, play the ball!" With his head bowed low and shoulders lowered, Aris approached his mother and took the ball. "Good," she exclaimed, with a squinting smile, and looking at me, and at him, she once again instructed, "Play the ball!" When she went back inside, we drifted off to the center of the yard, where I tossed the ball to Aris, who immediately dropped it. Sunken and listless, he reluctantly hoisted the ball over his head, and in an awkward and imbalanced way, barely pushed it over to me. I would slowly roll the ball or gently toss the ball back to him, as carefully as possible, not saying a word. He was so limp and reluctant to play. Nevertheless, we "played the ball" for as long as it took to acceptably say that, at least, we tried.

As far as I can remember, we never played those games again. From then on, I preferred to play at my home and with other friends. But even then, I felt a loss where Aris was concerned, and this was because there was something different about Aris, something I could sense but not put my finger on, something present but undefinable, something baffling. Perhaps he did not know what it was either, or perhaps he knew and would not say, so that there was a hidden, secret about Aris that I was not privy to. All I knew was that something was wrong. I just couldn't place what it was. And that's how we left things from then on. We were close, but only so close.

In the course of time, we would serve at the altar and attend youth group and choir together. We would share all kinds of experiences and form a whole social fabric of life. Yet, despite all we had in common, we inexorably drifted apart. Although we would meet in high school and share engaging encounters afterward, things were never the same again. We would even spend hours talking about issues of love, faith, and the big relevant social issues of our day, but there was a place, an interior to which I was restricted, a place that he would not show me, where I could not go, a place I could not even imagine. That's where we settled for years to come.

Suffice to say that I began with a best friend, and I believed that I still retained a best friend, but the reality was that I began to lose him from then on, at first gradually and then with wider and wider divergences. Despite our many personal achievements throughout our lives—for instance, Aris would

THE Fablehood TRILOGY

become prominent as a dedicated Army Chaplain, a sharp businessman, a compassionate counselor, and as a person of exquisite taste—a mysterious gap grew between us, one that neither of us wanted nor knew how to remedy. I knew he had a private issue, and so did he—and I am sure that I knew what it was—but there was not much either of us could do about it. No matter how we hoped or tried, we were never able to put the issue aside or reconcile ourselves. We would never again be as close as we were as children. I guess some currents are just too strong, just too unyielding, to avoid eventual drifting apart. But I shall always remember him with the greatest fondness one friend can have for another. May his memory be eternal.

CHIP 16: *Gain and pain are rooted in the nearness of love. This is especially true when one is discovering themselves, for nothing is so disquieting, nay, disruptive than the emergence of the Self. The surprise traits, the personal blemish that cannot be powdered over, the knowledge that you are somehow different, that you are in society but do not have a place there—these are all hidden pains of emerging as a unique person. So it is, then, that childhood innocence cannot bear the terrifying aspects of maturity, especially when it must shoulder the heartbreaking of private suffering. Gain and pain are rooted in the nearness of love.*

17

Unexpected Cheesecake

The door was always open at our home, or so it seemed. Folks were always just dropping by, most often without a call or any notice. There was a comforting communal sense when folks came over. And they were always at the house. My mother should have charged a fee for her very generous and flexible open-door policy and valuable counseling. Instead, there was always some food, some nuts, grapes, fruit, always something on hand to feed the daily wayfarer. And, of course, when her barrage of villagers came by, they rarely just came and went. No, most would liberally spend hours of my mother's time, which she received gracefully and sweetly. There were, however, some folks who were almost always brief in their visitations. One of these pilgrims was my godfather, Sam Fokas.

When Uncle Sam visited, I alone had the privilege to call him *"Nouno,"* Greek for godfather. He was always very animated and exaggerated in his gestures, that is, wide eyed and with his hands gesticulating constantly. Ironically, while, on the one hand, his physical manners were dramatic, his voice, on the other hand, was soft, like two feather pillows. I enjoyed him stopping by, but I was not sure whether his animations were real or pretend. Of course, it did not matter, since he was making the effort to stop by and keep in touch with my parents, and with all of us kids. Now, however, I realize that he was being kind and attentive, and his sweetness was genuine. And speaking of sweetness, he would often come over with the most delicious non-Greek item possible. He would bring a large brown box, tied with string, as if bandits were out to steal the morsel within. Unraveling the wrapping, the box lid would be lifted to reveal a creation I have always associated with my godfather—the New York cheesecake. I never knew where he bought it, but I was over the top every time he arrived with one. By the way, ever since those enjoyable dessert days, I have always preferred cheesecake rendered in the dry New York style, as opposed to the creamy expression popular everywhere else. And then, no sooner had he revealed his delicious offering, he was off and about. What perfect timing! I always loved his artful visits: short, to the point, not overbearing or self-indulgent, never nosy or pushy, just delightful, and, of course, delicious!

    Visits from my *nouna*, that is, my godmother, were the complete opposite. When she came, like so many of the other women, my mother would have to clear out hours for her, which again she did without complaint. Kyria Mitsa (Lady Demetria) was constantly giving, constantly. My *nouna*, Rosie, was a truly sweet and loving woman, who often wore bright red lipstick and carried herself with a deportment fully in the middle age of life. She would stand by the

Unexpected Cheesecake

counter, or by the kitchen table, as she watched my mother at work with her innumerable and unending chores. As if she were at the psychotherapist office, my *nouna* would talk on and on. I can still hear her rather raspy voice, as she would say, often several times during her prolonged stays, "Ach, Mitsa, what are we going to do? That's life. Ach!" And the same would be said in Greek, always with a plaintive and resigned tone. I could never figure out why she was so continually unhappy, but my mother never seemed to wonder about that. Instead, she would nod and listen, always with patience and a kind smile. And this kind of "conversation" would go on week after week, with patient upon patient, her friends.

Of course, the children of her friends became mine as well. The children of my godparents were no exception to this rule. They had Cindy, Dino, and Maurice, and very often I was invited to "stay over" at their house. We all played their many games and sat up to watch "Leave It to Beaver" and "The Brady Bunch," and whatever else was on their beautiful console TV. They had a fun and playful home, where I always felt at such ease and secure. Funny how it is, though, when you sleep in someone else's bed and encounter the odd odors and weird stuff other homes have. My godparents were certainly most accommodating, and I do not write to criticize. But, whenever I entered the home and went through the living room, I was readily struck by the industrial scent of thick protective plastic that thoroughly wrapped every piece of furniture in the room. (Incidentally, many of the Greek ladies plasticized their furniture this way; my mother did not). No one ever sat in the living room, with its supremely protected chairs and couches, its

THE Fablehood TRILOGY

gilded frames, velvet wallpaper, and jangly crystals. However, I always made sure that I stopped and studied an odd lampstand, which was uniquely adorned. With a female figurine holding the lamp up, fishing lines descended from the head to the toe, each line soaked with rolling beads of oil. Illuminated by the lamp-bulb, the oil glistened in its endless exercise in futility, I have never seen a lamp like that before or since, but if I ever do, I will honor my godparents with good memories and gratitude for their enduring kindness to my family and myself.

By the way, years later, when I was an adult, just for fun, I drove over to their 1960's house. I arrived unannounced but was warmly received, nonetheless. We sat together, godparents and me, and we enjoyed our *parea* (Greek for "company, fellowship") together. We had cheesecake and coffee. And I did not stay too long.

CHIP 17: *A small slice is preferable to an entire pie. Brief and frequent is better than occasional and drawn out. To wit, we benefit most when we can see one another more often, with short visits, with bursts of flavor, rather than rarely and gorging for a long time. A small slice is preferable to an entire pie.*

18

Brotherly Angst

In the original *Star Trek* series, the main characters are set apart by their predominant personality traits. Hence, Mr. Spock portrays a cool thinking, logical person, while Dr. McCoy embodies the oversensitive emotional type. The character who balances these extremes is, naturally, the celebrated Captain Kirk. In every episode, we witness the surefire captain, during some life-threatening debacle, being advised from both sides. He adroitly sifts and synthesizes all the necessary information, and once again, week after week, makes the appropriate decisions for the dire needs of the Starship Enterprise and her crew of over four hundred (whom, of course, we never actually see).

Well, on my mother's side of the family, the personalities seemed to fall in a prescribed line, as if designed by the creators of *Star Trek*. However, we entertained some rather ironic variations to the Human/Vulcan theme. For example, I think that both of my uncles considered themselves as Captain Kirk,

THE Fablehood TRILOGY

but in reality, that billing was always my mom's to play. The youngest of the siblings, Uncle George, was clearly Dr. McCoy. He was an emotionally explosive actor, while the eldest of the siblings, Uncle Danny (Damianos in Greek), was the sage-like and ponderous Mr. Spock. These designations left my mother, naturally, as the one to find the middle road and the only one providing a sane and peaceful way forward, one that would keep everyone talking to one another. Her brothers, my uncles, were each in their own ways difficult to handle, each insisting that they were right about an issue, and neither yielding an inch to the other. Without getting into an argument or raising her voice, my mother was able to keep the balance, which I consider a small miracle. This she accomplished by relying upon her ability to express wisdom in gradual diplomatic, and ego-saving, steps, never too passive nor too aggressive. I have yet to meet a more effective mediator. I can only lament that the Middle East Peace Process did not employ a certain Mitsa Manuel. Anyone who could find the golden mean between two such opposing and hardheaded pillars would be worthy of the noblest of Nobel prizes.

Consider the challenge she faced. In truth, I would be hard pressed to find two brothers anywhere who could be more opposite than these two. Each lived in the not-so-bustling city of Reading, Pennsylvania, and each worked in the food industry. But that was all they had in common. So, when they would venture from that great urban center of Reading, we would witness how very different they were, like two ends of a battery, each carrying its own potent charge, and each dangerous.

Brotherly Angst

Uncle George was the more luminescent and electric of the two. He would be on the positive end, hyperexcited and in a whirl about this or that food or person or event or accomplishment—particularly by his children—to be the best or the most. Positively charged, Uncle George could never stay in any place too long. As my Aunt Esther would say, "He's got ants in his pants." Uncle George was given over to immediate and reactionary rants and exaggerations. Loud, demonstrative, and assertive (some might say pushy), no one, upon meeting Uncle George, ever forgot the encounter. And I could easily understand why, what with his George Clooney good looks, his delightful Greek accent, and his unbridled passions he could, and would, talk your ear off, and, even if you held a completely different point of view, you would fall in love with him during the whole tirade. As a *maître d'*, Uncle George was suave and debonair, as if Cary Grant was taking care of your table and directing you to the best of the menu. He was compelling, charismatic, and the most dynamic person in every room. And, he also considered himself to be the best looking (he was usually right about this one), and certainly right about everything. Of course, he was not always right, and in fact, he was quite often wrong. He despised when these failings were clearly explained to him. I can still hear how my mother would calmly and serenely disagree, always with logic and a *sotto voce*, even as he would rant even more. These epithets and verbal rantings would be peppered with such articulations as, "TZeesus Krist, Mitsa, Don't you have eyes!" Enjoying the tussle, Uncle George would spew and hurl out such invectives, and lob out such verbal mortars, that my mother could only respond to such gusto with a smile that was pacifying and eased the tension. Then she would balance the score with him. The truth is, of course, that we all loved his histrionics, almost as much as he did! His visits were almost journeys to *terra incognita*, "places unknown," but certain of one thing: it was going to be a dramatic venture, wonderfully accompanied, with gifts of every kind. He would bring all kinds of goodies, raise up some kind of little ruckus, and, just as we were all settling in, he would be off and away again. I can hear him now, barking at his bride, my Aunt Shirley, "Come on Seerley! Pahmeh! We've gotta go. Close your mouth now. Tzeesus Krist!" And off they would go! May his memory be eternal.

Uncle Danny was the complete opposite. Everything about him was slower, more deliberate, cautious, measured, and had a different tone. Uncle George spoke in a high pitch, as if he had to find a bathroom right away. Uncle Danny's voice was deep, bass, much slower and purposed, and brooding, like thunder from the depths. When he came to visit, Uncle Danny would park himself in a comfy chair or on a long couch, and settle in for the day. While Uncle George was on the edge of the kitchen seat, Uncle Danny fully occupied the setting. Not as attractive as his counterpart, Uncle Danny made up for his lack of exterior beauty with an encyclopedic wealth of knowledge. Moreover, he would make a statement with complete and utter confidence, as if his knowledge could not, in any way, be suspect. He was right, and that was it! There was never a doubt or debate; Uncle Danny was logical, thorough, experi-

Brotherly Angst

enced, and authoritative. Sanguine, settled, resolved, when Uncle Danny told you a fact, he was right, no questions asked, except, of course, except...when he was wrong. And, as he would remind my mother, in clear and concise Greek that I could not understand, how she could not possibly be right. I remember, for instance, the whole debate regarding the year of my mother's birth. My mom said it was 1932. No, my Uncle corrected her; it was 1931. This went on and on for hours, until my mother, with her usual wisdom, would say, the date does not matter, thus thwarting any more debate on the issue. And so, this kind of dialogue would simply continue, with the result being that it would come to an end by Uncle Danny falling asleep on one of the couches.

Looking back, I have to admit that he truly was a wealth of information, and I regret that I was not old enough to ask relevant questions, or, for that matter, that I could even discern meaning from his goblin-esque Greek accent. But his resource was not lost on me as a child. I say this because, even then, I could sense that I was not just talking to a middle-aged man displaced in America, but rather to an ambassador from another time and place. When I saw him, I witnessed the bucolic island of Kos under the bootstrap of German troops, the struggle to get by and survive, the hunger, the fear, the loneliness, and the escape to the West—America and the promise of untold opportunity. So much history, so much suffering set deep within, far from me, and asleep on the couch. May his memory be eternal!

How two people, so completely opposite, could be raised by the same parents is a testimony to the

THE Fablehood TRILOGY

power of individual personalities. Genetics is an amazing study. Clearly, they had their own genes, and thank God for the differences. But honestly, having the two of them in a room at the same time was simply exhausting, if not, as Mr. Spock would say, "Fascinating."

CHIP 18: *"Pan metron ariston." Everything in moderation. The middle way is often the wisest. But the extremes are rather attractive as well! The middle of the road is the best part to travel on. But the far sides provide adventures of their own. But for the sake of sanity and clarity, stick to the heart of the road. "Pan metron ariston." Everything in moderation.*

19

Makrothimia

I never heard them complain, not once. Stoic to the point of ossification, my aunts on my mother's side, were portraits of *makrothimia*, a delightful Greek word that translates to "long-suffering." And indeed, they were. Although these women were both so outwardly different, they bore the common cross of supreme patience.

Aunt Shirley was Uncle George's wife. She was a glittery starlet, who could not help but ooze her white American pedigree. She reminded me of Elizabeth Montgomery from *Bewitched*, and I often thought she was much prettier than anyone on television. She was supremely well-adorned with the modish fashions of the seventies, but on the well-appointed formal side, with bright dresses, wide lapels, hair coiffed perfectly to frame her lovely Miss America face. She would have fitted in perfectly at a country club or at a high society soiree. Always smiling, pleasant, and sweet, Aunt Shirley was a striking and beautiful woman, even to a kid like me. And I was proud to have a genuine true-blue, blue-blooded American in

THE Fablehood TRILOGY

our family, although I always wondered what it must have been like for her. She never revealed what was churning on the inside. Instead, like all grand women of her time, she kept herself composed, tight-lipped, and well-heeled. I could only imagine what it was like to be married to such a lady's man like my Uncle George. He was the guy you would take to the casino or to the racetrack, and so I could not imagine how that all worked. After all, she was much more "White House" than playhouse, and her bearing exuded such grace. In any event, none of us were privy to what was under the hairspray and makeup, and perhaps it was better that way. All I know is that she always treated my siblings and myself with great kindness.

Aunt Irene was Uncle Danny's wife. She was a traditional Greek homemaker, and her dress and demeanor reflected her more conservative outlook. She seemed accustomed, or perhaps, comfortable, not to draw too much attention to herself. Oddly, like her husband, Aunt Irene ("Irini" in Greek), was often difficult to understand. Her voice felt as if it were emerging from a cellar in her throat, cloistered, measured, tip-toed, ever cautious not to say something "wrong," whatever that may have been. Dour, shy, private, Aunt Irene, just like Aunt Shirley, also kept her feelings and viewpoints "close to the vest." I was accustomed to my mother, who spoke out easily and warmly, and the rather loud and opinionated women on my dad's side. Her silence was somewhat curious, if not, baffling to me. Without sounding the least bit disrespectful, she reminded me of the Great Sphinx of Giza: quiet, subdued, and hiding some mystery within. As with all of my family, Aunt Irene treated me and all my siblings with gentleness and kindness.

Makrothimia

But, oh my, it must have been difficult being married to my all-knowing Uncle Danny. I can only imagine how they spoke to each other, and what they would have discussed. Hmm. Who can understand such things as marriage?

Although different in cosmetics and culture, Aunt Shirley and Aunt Irene nonetheless shared a common experience. They both kept their inner selves hidden, though I am not sure why. Perhaps that was the modus operandi for wives in those days, or perhaps it was wiser to hide, lest anyone be too critical or gossip. I suppose that I was spoiled with my mother, who seemed to err on openness rather than secrecy. I think of them fondly now, but with an extra sense of compassion, empathy for the long-suffering they must have endured, the apparent call for a form of patience that I never knew, nor ever will, but will honor with love and respect.

CHIP 19: *No cry can ever be completely muffled. There is a suffering that does not involve blood or violence, but rather, sobs quietly and silently beneath the surface of the skin. And, sadly, there is no cosmetic that can cover it completely. The soul will find its cavern in which to wail, no matter what. No cry can ever be completely muffled.*

20

Trips to Trips

Back in my earliest of times, a drive from Lancaster to Reading, some 30 miles on old Route 222, was considered an epic journey for my dad. Perhaps it was due to his obvious reluctance or his simple disinterest or fear of travel. Whatever it was, the distance between these humble cities in south-central Pennsylvania was exaggerated whenever we ventured to meet my mom's family. Had we driven by horse and buggy, we might have gotten to see my Uncle George's and Uncle Danny's families sooner. The pace was not merely slow, but grudgingly elephantine, such that our nerves were already frayed by the time we reached our destinations (never a good sign). In a bow to childhood submission, I had sadly grown accustomed to this ride being an all-day affair. On our returns, we witnessed farms and even an old green dinosaur at the Sinclair gas station that we passed each time. As I lay my head down on the back seat, I recall the thumpity-thump-thump-thump of the road home, as I drifted off to sleep.

Trips to Trips

While on our visits, I kept to myself and my little world. And so, as a kid, I did not involve myself in the world of adult dialogue. All those napkins and tablecloths, coffee and cookies. Ugh! I found the whole affair of the grown-up world drab and uninspiring. No one ever seemed to play or have fun, just hours and hours of droning conversation, and for what? God only knew! And then, eventually, someone would get upset and the evening would come to a screeching halt on some slighted dramatic note. Who needed all of that when you could play with an Etch-A-Sketch or put photo wheels into a viewer and snap away at your leisure? I felt so much safer with the munchkin set!

Speaking of whom, the Tripolitis kids were divided into two cousin groups: the Uncle George/Aunt Shirley home and the Uncle Danny/Aunt Irene home. Oddly, we never all seemed to play together, at least I cannot remember doing so. In any event, we had a ball getting together, though in very different ways. The Uncle George/Aunt Shirley home, on the one hand, looked as if the Brady Bunch was going to descend the stairs at any time. Even the neighborhood had that idyllic bike path and white-picketed fences so often popularized on television. The Uncle Danny/Aunt Irene home, on the other hand, had the patina of an older, comfortably settled stone/brick row home appeal.

In the former home, my cousins were John, Linda, and Georgia, and in the latter, the cousins were Joyce and Mary. With no disrespect intended, I played almost exclusively with John, and rarely, if ever, with my female cousins. The girl cousins

THE Fablehood TRILOGY

were lovely in every way, and winners in their own worlds—especially later in life, in the academic and professional fields—but I had no clue how to play with them. They were like little goddesses, each of whom could sing like angels and dance like butterflies. Joyce was the eldest and seemed to be light years ahead of me, and even the rest of the girls seemed more mature than me. (It must have been me, then!) They also possessed tremendous energy and sass, but I could not find a bridge beyond my deep admiration for them. In fact, I thought of them, and still do, more with honor, more as sisters than as cousins. And so, while we were close, we just did not play together.

My cousin, John, however, was much easier with similar play interests. He was simply a blast! Of course, I was closest to John because we were both boys, and as a child, that is a big deal. We got along swimmingly. Perhaps this was because our mutual parents would not have had it any other way. Consequently, we all feel the same way to this day. John seemed to bend over backwards to welcome us with his gentlemanly grace. I always admired the genuine kindness and generosity in his soul.

As a child, John had the best and the newest of all of the games and gadgets. If there was a new game or a fancy item, he had it, and he would readily share all of his fun entertainment with ample enthusiasm. He was so generous and inviting, so unlike most boys his age. His kindness defused any hint of jealousy that I might have easily justified toward him. The same has held true for all my cousins, who were all graced with the same generous spirit. Indeed, I have been rooting for them all my life. John's humor would also crack me up, as he would chuckle at his own jokes. I recall, for instance, when he would joke about his last name, "Tripolitis," guffawing over this line: "Better be careful, or 'Trip' 'will' 'eat-us.'" Ok, maybe it was a little weak, but it had good mileage back then.

John was not only the very picture of cool, but he had the added attraction of not taking himself too seriously. A year older than me, John seemed to ooze confidence and to know everything. He was handsome as a child, smiling and sparkly eyed. Later in life, he looked a little like a cross between Martin Sheen and Tom Cruise, with a touch of Rob Lowe tossed in for good measure.

But what I remember most about John was his ability to step aside willingly from the material items, shiningly tempting for me, to sing Disney songs instead. We would croon, him on pitch, and me searching for the words. After each attempted "song," we would laugh and tell stories together, sharing a space and time that I will treasure forever.

John would go on to play saxophone and love music of all kinds, and even marry a girl with the same name as my bride, Karen. Still close, and still crazy after all these years, John has always retained his jazzy cool.

As you can probably tell, I deeply admire my cousins, who are more like siblings in my heart than any other designation. We do not get together often anymore, as we live in different areas of the country, but we are all tremendously grateful when a special event, like a wedding or baptism, brings us all together. I am constantly amazed at how the children of our immigrant parents all turned out to be honorable and faithful people. They all remain true to the

THE Fablehood TRILOGY

Orthodox Church, even under many difficult circumstances, and they are all hardworking and marvelous people. There must have been something wonderful in that Tripolitis DNA! I thank God for such wonderful cousins.

CHIP 20: *Blood can be enriched by water. Blood relatives do not have to remain relatives. They can even be people you admire, people you want in your life, people with whom you choose to associate; relatives can even become friends. Blood can mix with water and be neither diluted nor saturated. Indeed, blood can be enriched by water.*

21

Manuel's Comet

Every 76 years or so, the world awaits Halley's Comet. Science has determined that pattern because the visitation follows precise mathematical models. Hence, a faithful astronomer can predict, with excellent certainty, the next visit, and the one after that, and then the next one, and so on. As a child, my family and I also experienced a kind of "Halley's Comet" event, but never with any predictable orbit or timing. Our stellar quasar was my parabolic brother, Steve, who would swoop in from time to time and regale us with stories of his travels and adventures.

A gung-ho marine, jauntily defending our country's freedoms, Steve was the first son of my father from his first brief marriage. Angular, lean, tightly wound, and ready to spring into action, Steve possessed the same facial and body dimensions of our mutual father. Steve, however, resembled Dad to a striking degree, the genetic material being freshest with the firstborn child. (His likeness to our dad was far more pronounced than with my siblings or myself.) With large eagle-like eyes, sharp jaw, and

THE Fablehood TRILOGY

a well-chiseled square chin, Steve, whom we called "Stevie," was the inheritor of most of Dad's potent DNA. Leaving high school to seek destiny in the Far East country of Vietnam, Steve could do no wrong in our father's eyes. For Dad, Stevie "hung the sun, the moon, and the stars," and his sporadic visits were always occasions of immense pride.

Stevie mystified me, since I really did not understand where he was coming from or to where he was going. Perhaps he did not know either, but he would keep us laughing and wide-eyed with his photos of some distant port, an admiral, a general, or even of the president. Even more entertaining were his risqué, and ever salacious imagery of various clothing-challenged nymphettes. We always wondered how he managed to convince these little birds to pose so prettily. I loved his racy and taboo subject matter, to which we all laughed, much to his delight. I could see the dramatic relief on Steve's face, as my parents would feign scandal, while chuckling all the while. I imagined that for such an experienced and wide-ranging journeyman, it must have been comforting to be in a home, a place where he was not only accepted, but also praised and admired. During an age of shifting sexual mores, with television and magazines so hormonally engorged, we all appreciated the candor with which Steve presented his purple material. In fact, I think we were all relieved that Steve was able to pull us all so overtly and blithely across the sexual dialogue line. His visits were like welcome needles, relieving pressure in the gonadic swells of our home. In other words, he was able to verbalize and illustrate the anxieties we harbored about sexual awareness. His humorous approach enabled each of us to cross our mute bridges of reservation. He was able to accomplish this because Stevie was free as a bird, and we loved him for it, because he offered us all a chance to escape vicariously. And so we did.

Though he called me "four eyes," and teased me mercilessly, I loved receiving attention from this warrior-prince-adventurer. Like a returning comet, his visits expanded our world, and brought us from Lancaster all the way across the Asian continent and to points around the globe. Intensely patriotic, Steve's passion to serve our nation in such a risky way raised my esteem for him. His visits became such great moments of celebration that my mom kept *kourabiedes*, Greek wedding cookies in store during the holidays to treat Stevie and other visitors. Indeed, over the course of time, when Stevie would enter the house, he would go right for the cookies and bypass all of us, just as a way to express his love and admiration for my mom. What a blessing to grow up with such a dashing jarhead of a brother. In the end, of course, his mission was complete—he liberated us, even while we enjoyed the comforts of home.

Later on, sometime during those years, Stevie would come home with a lovely woman by his side. Jaylene was blond, beautiful, and the most accepting, laid-back woman I had ever met. She would have to be, of course. Because, even with her present, Stevie would not hesitate to show us his slides—and without a scintilla of shame—one bikini cup at a time.

Four children later, and many more grandchildren to add to his brood, Steve went on to teach at the Pennsylvania State University in Happy Valley, and to be privileged as the staff photographer for the Nittany Lions. Not a bad place to land after 28 years

THE Fablehood TRILOGY

in the *Semper Fi*. He is still a great source, of my pride and admiration, and always will be.

CHIP 21: *A comet is never encountered without a gaping mouth. Some folks are comets. An impression does not have to take long to be truly impressive; It is the depth that matters, not the length. Like the sudden appearance of a deer in a yard or a dolphin from the beach, a shooting star, or even a soaring comet, can affect a person more in a moment than in a lifetime of starry nights. A comet is never encountered without a gaping mouth.*

22

One Giant Leap

We shared an event with millions of our closest friends. I would imagine that many were just like us, huddled together beneath blankets in their family TV rooms to witness what no one else in history had ever seen before. The whole family was gathered—parents on chairs, and we three kids sprawled out on the floor—to watch Apollo 11 land on the moon. And then, after the odd-shaped spacecraft lowered itself gingerly and a little of the dust had cleared, the door at the top of a stairwell opened. And out came a man in a bulbous white astronaut suit, covered from head to toe in anticipation for what his feet might feel when they reached the lunar surface. Hovering just for a moment, and then springing from one step to the other, the man made his way down the ladder. We all watched breathlessly, as if we were experiencing a dream or acting out some universal drama, as one man stepped forth for all humanity, as we gazed at the heavens and wondered. Finally, of course, with his footprints clearly visible in the dusty landscape, and with a brief second of muffled

THE Fablehood TRILOGY

transmission, the great man uttered those immortal words, "One small step for man, one giant leap for mankind." I remember feeling, at seven years old, on that evening of July 20, 1969, that we were all seeing the fulfillment of millennia of dreams, the fruit of tireless aspirations. The whole evening was so incredible that we could hardly wrap our minds around it. What did it all mean? Where would we go from here? What does God think of all of this? With all these questions and more whirling about in my head, I just had to get outside. We all did.

We just stood and craned our necks upward. Silent, drinking it all in, there we saw the old familiar moon, bright and shining in the summer air. And, if we looked closely enough, we even imagined our friends up there waving to us. We felt a sense of pride in being human and a sense of kinship with everyone in the world and beyond. The time was elevated, stalled for just a second—our lives had paused. We were keenly aware of where we were, and the historical moment before us. It was just a second, just a speck of time, just enough time to wave back.

CHIP 22: *Gild the passing of time. For a moment once lived will never come again, even one shared by billions of siblings. This is because eternity only occurs in the present. Gild the passing of time.*

23

Puff the Magic Father

None of us are simply black and white figures. There are more hues to us than meets the eye. My dad was the perfect example of this little truism. He was a man of many colors: bright and cheerful, during the day; but by night, after a few drinks, his soul would turn to shadows. His intoxicant of choice was the alcohol of the common man, the blue-collar beer. Owing to his early forays into delinquent imbibing, his addiction gained hold of him from an early age. As the years and the lagers accumulated, Dad experienced the change that a powerful drug, taken repeatedly, would assault on any human nervous system. By the time we came onto the scene, the transmogrification was well under way, and there was little that we or our long-suffering mother could do. We just had to learn how to time our interactions for the better hours of his daily cycle, and to avoid the uglier hours. I found little humor in such pat phrases as being "three sheets to the wind," as living with an alcoholic sucks the joviality from one's soul.

THE Fablehood TRILOGY

All I knew was that a wonderful person during the day would descend into a maddening ogre by night. There was no escape from this daily hell, the shadowy caves of my childhood.

The sadness of these daily changes has certainly etched a deep scar among all of us children. I can still recall how my mother, a wonderful cook, would bring out the most artfully crafted dinners, which he would tastelessly dust over with tablespoons of salt and pepper. Upon tasting the food, which he had just desecrated with his tacky spicing, he would have the gall to say, "This tastes like shit!" and then disgustedly storm up from the table. I felt so sorry for my doting mother, as she suffered to handle a man more akin to a brat than an appreciative husband. We all hated him when he acted like such a child, as we conveniently rationalized that his insufferable behavior was the result of the devil in the beer that was speaking, rather than the desperate rantings of the insecure man inside. Who knew or could fathom why Dad was the way he was. We did our best simply to deal with his insanity on an everyday basis. Each of us struggled with his rampant alcoholism, and we have each experienced every emotion from rage to rancor to resignation. During his life, he exhausted us. Now that he has passed away, thankfully, there are no more feelings of regret, at least for me.

But I would like to say that, even back then, during those difficult and trying times, Dad had remarkable moments of kindness. He could be downright sweet in his kindness, and maddeningly thoughtful. Every once in a while, he would reveal that the hurt

Puff the Magic Father

child he protected deep within himself, could manifest signs of a most compassionate man.

There were evenings, for example, when, after we were fast asleep in our beds, he would come to the door with a large Zangari pizza in his hand. To be awakened by the fragrance of this most delicious of Neapolitan pizzas is a memory I have always treasured. The only sleep-related memory that even comes close is recalling the joy of waking up to new fallen snow on a wintry morning. We would follow Dad like he was the Pied Piper to the dining room, where we would enjoy the best Italian delight that Lancaster could offer. I do not know how he thought of these occasional gastronomic awakenings, but the impression upon me, and all of us, has been permanent. To this day, my siblings and I search high and low to find a pizza even remotely like Zangari's. But honestly, I know it was the surprise of the late-night presentation that made it so beguiling. What a wonderful way to be awakened! He also, by the way, frequented another great junk food place called "Twin Kiss," where he would haul enormous cheese steaks and Italian hoagies to our waiting table. No wonder I have such a weakness for every food that is bad for me, as Dad did a great job instilling these frivolous delights in my siblings and me. In stark contrast to Dad, Mom would rarely waste money on food that she could make so much better, and less expensively, at home, But we embraced the waste with an unfair and imbalanced enthusiasm, since it was so endearing for us to see Dad in a much softer light. On a deeper and non-spoken level, I think we were each secretly pulling for Dad to do whatever he had to do to get out of

THE Fablehood TRILOGY

his drunken funk. And so, we readily supported him. Now the reader can see how confounding he was, crazy and rude and unbearable at times, and then, refreshingly surprising. A technicolor man! But there were more shades.

A couple of gestures he offered were just as delightful, perhaps even more so, since they had the benefit of being at regularly convenient intervals. Near the Buchanan Elementary School, and just behind the Wheatland Junior High School that we all attended, there was a marvelous candy and comic shop called "Ned's." Every week or so, Dad would take us to Ned's to pick whatever candy we wanted, along with the comics we chose to read. Dad was an ardent collector of comic magazines, and he loved to see the enthusiasm on our faces, as we packed our little brown bags with bazooka bubble gum, dots, jujubes, and the like, while hauling a week's worth of cartoon bubbles in the other hand. Candy was dirt cheap, and so were we! More importantly, this generously sweet act was quintessentially "Dad" too.

Then there was "Hammond's Pretzels," purveyors of the best hard triune baked goodies in all Amish-Menno Land. Just a little bakery, humbly set among brick row homes in the West End of Lancaster, Hammond's was a place Dad would take us to indulge in "Brokers," the fragmented leftover pieces of pretzels that you could get for a bargain. Within the arid warmth of the tiny hearth, you could feel the furnace blast of production, the well-crafted traditions of old German and American industry in the baking. Here was a place where the humble pretzel was elevated by know-how handed down from century to century. There was artful craftsmanship just breathing in the salty dry air, as we would consume the crunchy pretzels hot out of the oven. We loved these little pilgrimages! We loved them so deeply that to this day a visit to Lancaster must certainly include a stop at Hammond's. Dad had a love for all things delicious, immediate, and local, and for that my siblings and I are most grateful and appreciative.

Finally, yet another place we would regularly go was the public library, downtown on Orange Street and next to the Old Church of St. James. I loved the quiet civility of the library. "What a world," I thought. You could go into this place freely and without anyone looking over your shoulder, and page through any book or subject that you wanted. What freedom and advancement! The library is the epitome of civilization and serenity! What a concept! So, while we spent our time idling among stacks of books in the children's area and anywhere we pleased to capture our attention, Dad would peruse the books that were for sale in the basement—a dollar or so for a yard's length of books! Dad would get vast volumes of history, art, encyclopedias, all kinds of books, which we would subsequently soak in, to line the shelves in our home. I would spend many hours perusing these tomes, and I knew that all this transported knowledge came from his great love of learning. To this day, I love going to the library with its homey and civilized airs, offering volumes of better memories. In later years, I would go by myself to buy the same books for myself. Such wonderful experiences remain spectral rays of Dad's enduring memory.

THE Fablehood TRILOGY

CHIP 23: *Every mold is cast once. No one is cast in a single shape. We are all as complex and beautifully crafted as any of Michelangelo's sculptures. We each have rough hews and smooth polishes. Each sculpture is lovely and unique. Every mold is cast once.*

24

The Shop

"The Shop" was, of course, Dad's barbershop. His "home away from home," was situated on a side street in old row-home Lancaster. The barbershop was Dad's special hair clipping temple. Suffused with stale cigarette smoke and chilled to meat-locker cold, the shop was where Dad's faithful old tribe would come in to get buzz cuts and hear all about theology, politics, and current events.

The haircutting trade became my Dad's "bread and butter" after his stints with the U.S. Army, then a failed venture at boat design, and a short-lived placement with a big multi-chair barbershop. A high school dropout, Dad was determined to strike out on his own, and so that is, more or less, how the aptly named "Steve's Barber Shop" came about. The shop became his ticket to success, as Dad's pride rose with every head he snipped. I recall him saying many times, "If you have talent in your hands, you will always have gold." He meant this, of course, as a testimony to his God-given talent with his hands,

THE Fablehood TRILOGY

of which I possessed little to none. But Dad loved his little shop of clippers.

He held court there, and it was there that Dad exhibited his "public voice," his outward persona, the one he showed the world outside of our home. I was enthralled! Here, he was confident, in control, opinionated, gregarious, happy, smiling, and charismatic. At the shop, Dad was utterly charming, and so were his customers, I mean, "constituents." They were true blue "actual Americans," the kind we never saw at our house. They were the dominant people of the area, the prevailing culture so foreign from our Hellenic culture. These were the men, all white and Christian by the way, who fought in the two world wars and in Korea, and whose sons were caught up in a mess called Vietnam. These men were the "real" Americans, the ones who were elected to city councils, state and national legislatures, the true patriots in red, white, and blue. While we were tolerated, perhaps even accepted, as the happy go lucky Greeks, whom they fortunately did not disdain. They were White America, and we were Greeks, another hue entirely—olive, I suppose.

But, honestly, to my munchkin's eye, they seemed to be a thousand years old, and to me they truly looked the age. As the little squirt at the shop, I came to enjoy them; I came to appreciate the "gosh and by golly" camaraderie of the old farts, as they would tussle my hair, and welcome me into their private world. I was proud to be a brother in arms, a soldier who fit into their manly domain. Here was a place where all you needed to do was show up, and you immediately felt at home, no explanation necessary—like *Cheers*, where everybody knows your name. If

The Shop

you were there, then you belonged. And the freedom, well, here was a place where a guy could get almost anything he wanted, including a hot shave, a neck and shoulder massage, something to drink (coke in a tall glass bottle), cigarettes, and even a copy of *Playboy* magazine while you were waiting. (I also knew where Dad secretly stashed them.) I even enjoyed the old cash register, which I retain to this day, that would make a loud and dramatic ding whenever it was opened. How wonderful it was to be a subject in Dad's smoky realm. It was so different from home.

Naturally, when I was there, it was for my regular haircut, meaning invariably getting shorn, with a crew cut that would expose and "lift my ears" to an embarrassing level. My brother, George, much more vocal and stronger willed than me, came to eschew these forays to the shop, once he realized that he could get his hair "styled" and not merely "cut." He would go to a "salon," and his hair would be shampooed, cut, and even blow-dried, an entire process that was totally unheard of in "Steve's Barber Shop," with its traditional swirling tri-colored barber pole out front. While George was declaring his independence, seen as a kind of betrayal by my dad and his old farts' club, (Damn those mop-top Beatles and the rampage of '60's anti-establishment movements!), I could not move a finger or a toe. I shared neither George's passion for liberation from Dad's shears, nor the angst of the GI generation and their fears for the collapse of civil society. Moreover, I did not have the heart to disappoint my dad or feel like a Benedict Arnold to the boys' club there. And so, while I certainly admired George for his moxie, and I could readily understand his justification for moving on

THE Fablehood TRILOGY

from his allegiance to the shop, I just did not have enough anger or passion or whatever lower spheroids to declare myself independent of the crew cut look.

As time went by, George would stay with his same "stylist" for the next forty plus years, while I pretty much stayed with the Steve Manuel scissor treatment well into my twenties. Eventually, of course, all things change. The shop would later transfer from Sixth Street to our home on Millersville Pike, but in truth, the club was never the realm it once was. The barber pole stopped turning.

CHIP 24: *A snail without a shell is just a slug. We all need a place, a niche to live in. Every man craves his own castle, even if he must hang a barber pole out front to claim it. Likewise, every man needs to declare his own style, even if it means turning his back on the old and familiar. We crave to be ourselves. A snail without a shell is just a slug.*

25

Maternal Chairs

Once upon a time, there was a soft chair that was positioned in the corner of our living room. The "shoulders" of this piece were rounded, so that a person's shoulders could mold into its shape. One gray moody day, the lady of the house saw that the chair was alone and unoccupied, so she sat down on its supple seat. As the chair was positioned by a window, as well as in a corner, the lady could gaze outward from this position, while thoughts drifted and sifted through her mind. So, after her morning duties were completed, the lady would sit in the chair, where she would remain, while the man of the house was out, and the children were duly occupied. This she would do day after day, and month after month, observing the leaves on the trees changing from greens to auburns, the seasons coming and going, and the years passing by. The lady came to love her chair, and she sat in it, while faithfully maintaining her secret thoughts in it.

Many times, she would moisten the chair with her falling tears, so that she herself would think of it

THE Fablehood TRILOGY

as her personal weeping place. There she would ponder and pray and pour out her soul, and so the chair became blessed by her presence in it. However, one day, the lady, so deep in her thoughts and lost in her imaginings, forgot that she was weeping, and in the middle of the evening fell asleep in the chair. She was awakened by one of her children, who had gotten up to get some water and found his mother, sobbing in the twilight of the early morning. What could it mean, he wondered, and so he asked her. While drying the tears from her face, she mustered a smile, got the child his water, and sent him back to bed. She would assure him that she was just fine. Then, when she felt that she was once again composed, she would return to her chair. And the tears would continue to fall.

We all came to know and to honor "Mom's worry chair," where she would wrestle problems in her mind to seek solutions and peace. Sometimes, I would hear her muffled weeping and be able to make out the Greek words for money, *"chrimata,"* and *"Pos tha ta kanoume?"* for "How are we going to make it?" and *"Thee-ehh moo"* for "My God," and *"Panagia mou,"* for "All holy Virgin Mary." I knew not to interrupt her while she was on her chair, but I pined for her suffering, and wished with all my heart that I could take away her pain. I came to understand that she was worried sick about how we would survive, and this was her way to process the heaviness of life. *"Etsi einai E Zoe,"* "That's how life is," she would say, when pressed to explain her worry. Or she would say, *"Que sera, sera,"* "Whatever will be will be" in her native Greek, *"Ola einai grammena"* "It is already fated or written." There was no changing her thinking or moving her from the chair, and so my siblings

Maternal Chairs

and I would leave her alone. We knew that she needed her space, indeed, that she thrived on her personal retreats in the royal chair.

When we saw her in our normal times, and not furtively roaming around in the midnight hours, we always saw Mom smiling, pleasant, and full of vigor. If she wanted to be alone, that would prove to be rather difficult, as her many friends would descend upon the house, and the air would be filled with loud Greek banter. They occupied so much of Mom's time, coming over with all of their problems and woes, and would talk to her, as she played the role of willing counselor. They all knew that they were using her strength for their own, and they would admit as much, but for a little kid who would see his mother weeping at night, it all seemed so unfair. I wondered, who would be there for her?

To be sure, they were good, sweet women from the land of antiquity, and they desperately needed each other. They would occupy all the other chairs in the house, and each of them brought their own specific note to the harmony of my mom's friends. For instance, one of the women, "Thea (Lady/Aunt) Dionysia," was one of the truly entertaining ladies who would come to visit. One of Mom's oldest and dearest friends from the Isle of Kos, she would come over with her daughters Maria and Andrianna, with whom we are still friends, and no matter where we all went to play nor how deep into the long recesses of our thick-walled house, we could hear her laugh. Like the persistent harping of a hyena, her voice would wind its way across the distances and to our ears. We would have no idea what she was laughing about, but the memory of her charmed humor per-

THE Fablehood TRILOGY

sists to this day. Thea Dionysia and her gentlemanly husband, Harry, were a constant joy for my mom. I am so grateful.

And there were other women, occupying their own chairs at Mom's roundtable. One was "Thea Joannie," not from the old country at all, but a Massachusetts Greek, a different breed altogether. We kids enjoyed her, especially my brother, George, who admired how great she played the piano. Admiration of Aunt Joannie's flair inspired him to take on this mighty instrument. Her kids, Jamie and Julie, would become our playmates, but the real entertainment was just sitting in to listen to how Thea Joannie transformed normal English and simple Greek into a wonderfully irritating Bostonian accent. Her voice would transfer our Hellenism to wider, and yet unknown, shores. Sadly, poor Thea Joannie had a very troubled marriage, and even more drama with her children. Her chair near my mother was an enduring comfort for her.

Of course, there were many others who filled the chairs around my mother's counseling throne—Themis, Areti, Georgina, Presbytera Pearl, and on and on. They were all lovely people and most welcome in our home and filled the chairs most gracefully. Sometimes, when the weather was pleasant, they would all go outside to the front porch, which was covered over by thick grey flagstone. One of the women would bring an eight-track tape player, and then the bouzoukia and nasal Greek crooners would swoon to their hearts delight. Thea Georgina, my mother's late-night telephone-call friend, and my cousin Ginny would sit over where their cigarette smoke would not bother anyone, while the rest of

Maternal Chairs

the brood sat in iron-cast patio furniture all around the porch. Between sips of coffee and light banter, these delightful women would sing along with their featured performers. Their musical selections were mostly nostalgic, charged with romantic chords, reminiscent of the homeland. I recall, for instance, the "Trio Bel Canto," their smooth and unified harmonies, and their blue-tinted sounds of old and beloved Greece. The bouzoukia would sometimes strum in well-timed syncopated beats, and at other times in rapid bursts of musical excitement, accompanied by accordions and the soaring clarino, creating, to my young ears, melodies that seemed to spin in circles, creating whirls of joyous sound. The women would sing wistfully to these romantic scores, their heads waving back and forth to the rhythms, their eyes half-closed in reverie. The scene was hypnotic and intoxicating, so much so that even now, my feet are dancing to my memories of the movements.

I also recall the men, gathered separately around the yard or by Dad and his tractor, who would also come over and sing the old songs that cast their net in chords from afar. They would all be harmonizing together, without the slightest concern about who might hear them or what others thought. They were simply lifted upon a cloud of tuneful escape. Personally, I think these wistful, and absolutely beautiful songs, and heart-tugging ballads, were emotionally evocative even for the people who still lived in Greece. But for our extended family of friends, these nights were delightful vehicles to the shores and villages of Kos and Chios and all the lands of Hellas. These were firefly nights, illuminated by the candles each of the women held in their hearts for their native, and not

THE Fablehood TRILOGY

past, homes. I could not help but feel their heartfelt voices so openly and graciously shared in the evening air.

By the way, and I mean this with no disrespect to the memory of my mother, but on these evenings, while she could sing her heart out, Mom's voice was thankfully drowned out by the others in their wide circle. Poor Mom. Most of the time, she was flat and off-key, as if she were always singing the tilted descant to everyone else's faithful melody. Dad, however, had a deep impressive bass, and Thea Georgina had the sultry nasally voice of Greek women of those days, and with the others, they covered up Mom's musical deficiencies. Regardless of these limitations, Mom pressed on, loving those evenings and their nostalgic hymnody.

But, in the evening, in the quiet of the day's end, when everyone had gone back to their homes and their husbands and families, I knew where I could find my beloved mom. She would be in her chair, on her well-rounded throne, where she belonged. We would all leave her in her hushed solitude and with hope, finding the serenity that she so deeply sought.

As an addendum, my sweet niece, Elena Bruno, is the worthy recipient of this chair, as it now sits regally in her living room, somewhere in a corner. I have the lawn furniture on a patio in my backyard. Here, then, was the blessing of chairs! All that is missing now is an eight-track music player and a gaggle of crooning women.

Voltas

CHIP 25: *We all have a place at the table, our own special chair. The royal ones earn their thrones, and all the ladies and gentlemen in waiting benefit from their largesse. For not all of us sit at the head of the table. Some are more regal than others but make everyone feel at ease where they sit. But we all sit together. We all have a place at the table, our own special chair.*

26

Voltas

The countryside in Lancaster County was irresistible for anyone who loved nature, so Mom would toss my siblings and me into the car and take us for a *"volta."* A volta was the Greek equivalent of a walkabout—a ride, a Sunday drive, a trip to nowhere, a journey to journey, an opportunity to just get up and go out. We all loved these trips through the Amish farmland, miles and miles of nothing but farms and cattle, vegetable stands, fields of corn, wheat, tobacco, soy, farmers, and the horse-drawn plows and carriages to make this American pastoral possible. Or on another day, Mom would haul us down by the Susquehanna or Conestoga Rivers to view the broad expanses of water, and the folks who sported there. Of course, she was not just interested in the view, but here were some prime grape-leaf and greens picking territory. Even when we would get bored, as we often did, we knew that there was going to be a sumptuous reward at the end of our day's trekking. We knew that rich creamy ice cream

Voltas

was in the works, or maybe some pie at a restaurant, or something wonderful down the road.

Occasionally, we would stop by the side of the road, usually by some remote abandoned area, where Mom had previously sighted some dandelions or grape leaves or some other greens worth picking. As we would wait in the car, no matter the season, Mom would bend down from her waist and, with a knife in one hand and a bag in the other, she would harvest *"chorta,"* collecting native greens. Actually, the greens she loved the most were called *"vlastaria,"* which were wild mustard greens, which my mom had the uncanny ability to spot and harvest. She could drive along a road and home in on them from a distance. Many of the Greek women envied her for this culinary focus. In any event, *chorta* was the Greek equivalent of American collard greens— wild, abundant, and delicious, provided they were prepared correctly. And prepare them well she did! These captive greens would be cleaned and trimmed, and later boiled in water, to be finished off with some olive oil, vinegar, salt and pepper, and lemon. Simply fabulous! As a child, I could not stand this green stringy stuff, but now, as an adult I cannot imagine how I could have been so closed-minded. *Chorta* is amazing!

On other occasions, Mom would drive us about but end up at some Amish "Good and Plenty" or some "Smorgasbord," where we were treated to our hearts' delight. Over time, or perhaps just by habit, Mom settled on breakfast brunch places for her surprise destinations. Among her favorites was a place, not too far from our home, called "The Willow Valley Inn." Nestled in a little dale, framed by Weeping Willows,

THE Fablehood TRILOGY

appropriately leaning over a babbling brook and an old, covered bridge, the restaurant featured wide window seats, where we could eat our breakfast and gaze appreciatively. I loved that she thought of us so generously and treated us to a meal and a place that we really did not need nor deserve. Mom just wanted to show love in the best way she knew, by food, yes, but also by food that we went out and bought and enjoyed at a restaurant. She knew just how to treat us as *"kommati malama,"* "pieces of gold." When Karen and I were in the busy life of raising our kids, we took many *voltas*. Thank you, Mom! You gave us the extra mile, and that has made all the difference.

CHIP 26: *The side road is the compelling one. Be sure to take an occasional road trip to nowhere. On your return, you will find that you have been to somewhere memorable and renewing. Take a trip and do not be afraid. It is the drive that matters. Or, to quote the inimitable poet, Mr. Frost, "Take the road less taken." The side road is the compelling one.*

27

Wallywood

Naturally, since a little ride is pleasant, a bigger one should be much, much more pleasant, right? So it would seem to my Yiayia and our extended family and friends, that when Yiayia said, *"Elate, Pame sto Wallywood,"* – "Come, Let's go to Wildwood (a beach town in New Jersey), all the eager ears were listening. All the eager ears, of course, but Dad's. He would have nothing to do with going anywhere, especially somewhere as distant as the Jersey Shore. Four hours away! Four whole hours! What if we got lost?! And so, Dad absented himself from our extended *voltas* and vacations. We would have to go it alone, but not quite. If one part of the family was going, why then, everyone would have to go. And, just for the fun of it, why not invite friends as well? So what would start as a little extended *volta* became a migration of Greeks across state borders.

Four hours! Who ventures that far in a car without stopping for a picnic? That had to be the thought process going through Yiayia's brain, as we would travel over the Delaware Memorial Bridge, obviously

THE Fablehood TRILOGY

in dire need to stop at a rest stop after only two hours on the road. We would need a feast, of course, because with our family, and my Aunt Esther's family, and the Hazangeles family, all on board in various cars, we would certainly need sustenance. Baskets would tumble over each other with all kinds of Greek foods, breads, sandwiches, drinks, desserts, fruits, a meal set for a king, or perhaps a raving band of gypsies. After what felt like an interminable delay, we would get back on the road again, praying that we would not lose our way in the wilderness called "New Jersey." Eventually, we would meet up at our appointed motels, with their efficiencies and cloudy pools. We would begin to settle into our tiny rooms, miraculously fitting eight, where the place was designed for no more than four. We were expert at the half-truth where the management was concerned, saying we were one size group, when we were clearly another. We must have paid them off well with food, because we were never really bothered.

In the mornings, we would have to eat a massive breakfast, and then take the requisite hours to properly prepare ourselves to get to the beach, only to be scorched by the sun, which was by now at its highest and most dangerous point. No matter, there was always the stale-smelling pool to wade in and cool off.

Besides, it was the night activities that really counted most at Wildwood. Yes, here we displayed our best behavior, especially when playing the storied links of "miniature golf." The evening started off in that lovely twilight cool at the end of a day at the beach. With your body singed by the sun, nightfall and its refreshing dew was welcome relief, indeed. The perfect ending to such a day was, of course, a round of putting little balls in and around various artfully adorned holes. Who wouldn't love an evening like that? My siblings and I, along with Maria Hazangeles (Connie's teen friend), and her sister Andrianna (a good friend as well, but more George's age), paired off for a fun evening on the greens. We chose our putters and our colored balls, along with the all-important scorecard since, after all, there had to be a winner. And I was determined to be that winner!

We weaved and wended our way through the windmill, the clown, the lighthouse, and many other intimidating impediments, finally reaching the end of our game when it was time to tally up. I heard them all chuckle with their scores. Hmm, I thought, those scores are so shamefully low. So, I went up to them and announced, "Ha! I am the winner! See, my score is the highest!" One of the girls, I am not sure which, had the nerve to tell me, directly and smugly, that I had lost. She said, "You didn't win! The lowest score wins. You were the worst!" Not putting a lid on my rage, I went over to the little rental booth, where they kept the putters and balls, and grabbed as many putters as I could. As I held up one of the putters in a threatening gesture, I pronounced again, "No! I won!" And they retorted, this time laughing uncontrollably at my idiocy, and said, "Just accept it. You lost! God, you're such a spoiled brat!" (Which, of course, I was.) I'd show them, I thought! I then chased them down the boardwalk, with fire in my lungs and tears in my eyes. I'd show them all right, as I tossed the putters at them and hurled golf balls in their direction, missing them all completely. When I ran out of putters, I just ran as fast and as violently as I could until, finally, I was too exhausted to continue. I could scream, and that also worked well. Eventually, seeing me in tears, and realizing that the scene was as ridiculous as ridiculous could be, George and the girls finally stopped laughing. They returned to get me and take me home, even though they still managed to retain little smirks on their faces, and laugh among themselves, courtesy of the little brat they had to put up with. Not everything at the beach was suntan lotion and crashing waves. Sometimes you discover the surging volcanoes just below your own surface, a hot-tempered reality that I would have to learn to control, if ever I was going to grow up.

But I think that was definitely going to be awhile, given that I did not fare much better at the actual beach itself. With a yellow streak running down my back, I made sure that I would not venture any further than the water's edge. Why, might you wonder? Quite simply, the waves terrified me. Connie and George, and many others, often tried to encourage me to "just go out a little deeper." They would say, "Look, it's no big deal, we're just going to jump over the waves." Okay, I'll try. So, they held my hand and led me a little bit deeper with each step. Not so bad, I thought. But no sooner had I gone past the first breaker, when another one came up, rose over my head, and shoved my face deep into the sand. I came up, gasping, my mouth full of bitter seawater, my nose and eyes stinging from the assault upon them. I ran out of their grasp, crying, screaming, making a complete idiot of myself, and vowing that I would never allow myself to be fooled like that ever again.

I was nobody's fool! After all, I had already witnessed what happened to my brother, George, when he said that he was just going to go past the waves

Wallywood

(God forbid), and he would be right back. He went out a little bit, and it was fine, but then he disappeared behind what else, white caps! He did not come right back. And he was never going to! I could not see him. He was gone forever! I knew that the ocean had swallowed him up. I shrieked in terror. "The waves took my brother! The waves took my brother!" I could not see him. He was gone! And then, just before I might go thoroughly berserk, miraculously, he showed up! I was dumbfounded. George said, "You couldn't see me because of the waves. You see, I'm back. I'm here. I would not leave you. Relax!" But his words of consolation could not fool me. I refused to trust the ocean or the waves. So, I resolved to go no further than the water's edge.

But the wide expansive beach of Wildwood was no picnic either. With the metallic blue-grey of the sea on one side, and the amber desert of the sands on the other, this was a baffling and confusing place. Somehow, as I wandered along the perimeter of the shore, I repeatedly got lost, and I mean, terribly lost. I was totally flummoxed by this bedeviling place. It all looked monstrously the same. The waves, the towels, the umbrellas, the folks with white gunk on their noses, the lifeguards staring out from castles in the air, the families of children, mothers with bags of food, teens with radios, folks slurping drinks, the boats, the shimmering water, the endless sands—Oh, the utter confusion of it all! Thousands of places that all looked the same, so that no matter where I wandered, I would not find my people. I went just a little way, and it was as if the tide took me miles down shore. I cried out for my brother and sister, my mom and dad, but I recognized no one, not a single soul.

THE *Fablehood* TRILOGY

I spoke heatedly, desperately to anyone who would listen, and invariably some kind soul would lead me to the heroic lifeguard station, where there was a waiting area for lost souls like me. I got used to the frequent Jeep rides to the base, and my family grew accustomed to my meanderings, knowing where and how to find me, not if but when, I would go wayward. Alas, for the water! Alas for the Saharan beach!

For obvious reasons, I was always so grateful when we could be done with our so-called "beach vacations," and go home. Most of the joy of the trip, I came to learn, was in the anticipation of it. In fact, being there, squeezed like sardines in an olive oil can of a room, sounded better in preparation than it was in reality. The beach: there was the sand, the sun, the burns, the hurts, the getting lost among the crowds, the waves that could kill you, the jellyfish, the itchy crotch from salt and sand, the meanness of brother, sister, and their friends, and the distance of the grown-up world. Who could not enjoy all of that? Was it worth it? I suppose so. We wailed and whined until we could go back the following year. I am not sure how or when I ever transitioned to liking the beach, but it would not be during my formative years, for sure. (Now, in one of life's ironies, I live in a place called "Virginia Beach.") But it was not all bad, really!

One of the few great joys I experienced at the beach, and that I still muse upon nostalgically to this day, was the pleasure of getting a slice of "Mack's pizza" on the boardwalk. With a paper-thin crust, crispy and firm, the pizza was the size of a catcher's mitt, as it flopped over the edges of a paper plate. A sweet tomato sauce and a combination of cheeses assured that the pizza would be memorable for a lifetime. It was so memorable, in fact, that just last year, my wife, Karen, and I ventured to the boardwalk at Wildwood, just for the fun of it, and I looked for one place, and one place only. There I found "Mack's Pizza" on its famous corner of the walkway. And, as I approached it, the sign on its door read, "Closed for the season." Maybe it's sweeter that way.

CHIP 27: *Never leave your vacation, even if you must go home. The world, with all its wonder and beauty, is discovered with one unnecessary adventure at a time, and blissfully recalled one memory at a time. Your mind is an enduring Coney Island. Never leave your vacation, even if you must go home.*

28

The Asklepeion Mom

On the ancient island of Kos, far up in the highlands, there is a vast temple complex overlooking the wine-dark sea and the lands of Asia Minor beyond. Dedicated to the god Asklepius, the temple served as a place of healing. The governing principle of this hospital was the idea that if a person could rest, have fresh air, exercise, and relieve his mind of concerns, then his soul and body would be on the way to wellness. Wellness, according to the physicians of that time, and in particular a certain Hippocrates, was the result of balancing the physical and the spiritual aspects of the human being. These were defined in terms of "humors," some four basic forces that determined the tilt and keel of a person. If all was even among these humors, then the person was well. Any imbalance of these conditions produced "illness." The physician's calling was to restore the ideal balance of these disparate forces within the person, hence, "wellness." This symmetrical accounting of the human condition did not limit itself to life in the temple, but was to be practiced at home, and

The Asklepeion Mom

it was best exemplified for those who could benefit from good health there. Thus, intelligently governed self-care would begin in the Asklepeion Temple, and would ideally affect not only the individual but also the home and the surrounding towns and villages. In the ancient times, these asclepion temples would be transplanted all over Greece, but we may assert that the art of healing was also passed down generationally. Somewhere down the line, the hands, coupled with the sensitivity of the heart and the wisdom of the mind, the art of healing was undoubtedly passed on, inherited by many physicians of souls and bodies, good doctors and sacred ones, including one I knew well: "Kyria Mitsa," my mother.

    I can vividly recall, for instance, getting ill with some earache, from which I seemed to always be suffering. Mom would lay me down on the couch, and she would come over with a spoonful of warmed olive oil, and pour the silky liquid into my ear, sealing it with cotton. Remarkably, either just by her gentle touch or by the means of the substance employed, I would soon begin to improve. Then the music and poetry would issue forth from her mouth. The pace and the meter of the poems were especially soothing (though the music was uniformly flat). When I could lift my head with surety, and without pain, she would give me a light meal of toast and butter, washed down with hot tea made pallid with milk or sometimes lemon. I could feel myself getting my strength back, and by the end of the day, she would make something that I really did not appreciate then, as much as I do now. She would scramble eggs in olive oil and oregano and present it in a sandwich with tomato and feta, something absolutely wonderful that I sneered at back then. But I would eat it, and surely, I would feel better. When she determined it was okay, she would send me outside to play, and then I knew that I was restored. Her hands, her touch, her eyes, her look, her voice, indeed her whole sway above and round about me, oozed healing.

But I did not get the heavy, serious treatment. That was reserved for Dad, when he would get sick with some kind of cold or sniffle. I was, therefore, privileged to see healing demonstrated in a way that utterly baffled and scared me. Dad would lay face down on a bed, and Mom would take little round cups, invert them, and fill them up with the smoke of a candle. These smoke-filled cups would then be placed all over Dad's back, forming a suction wherever they were applied. In a kind of comic extension, no matter how Dad would shake or move, the cups would stay attached to him, as if they were dancing on his back. At some prescribed time, perhaps when little red circles developed on the skin just beneath the cups, Mom would lift the cups, and they would give off this dramatic popping sound. Dad would ooh and aah with the apparent pleasure of this procedure, called *"vendouzes"* in Greek, which I saw with more fear than understanding. But, after the process was completed, there was no question in my mind that Dad was feeling better. Smiling, relaxed, and more pleasant than I could ever remember him, Dad would arise from the bed, refreshed and obviously better in body and spirit. Needless to say, I was astounded by my mother, "the Healer."

I am most grateful that I was able to witness these and many other remedies that Mom faithfully administered to keep us well. As a side note, Mom

The Asklepeion Mom

was never interested in superstitious or occultic practices, such as reading coffee grounds or discerning tarot cards, as was often the practice of some Greeks. She was always rational, logical, practical, and gentle in her practice as a healer, an inheritance certainly worthy of Kos and its long tradition of sound medicine. We are all the healthier for her fine medical acumen and good judgment. Someday, in her memory, I may even try that smoke-filled cup remedy!

CHIP 28: *Healing begins and goes on with the Healer's touch. Good health is a balance of the forces in one's life, and we are blessed when we have someone to help us keep this balance. We are assured by the wisdom of those who have gone before us. It is thus wise to heed what they say and advise. To be healthy, then, follow the healthy. Be ready to perceive when you are touched. Healing begins and goes on with the Healer's touch.*

29

Follow the Bouncing Note

The sad reality was that in my elementary years, I found it challenging to learn anything theological or spiritual in Sunday school, as it always seemed to be "dumbed down" to the lowest common denominator, that is, presented to appeal for those who did not really care. I did not blame the teachers, as I could see this was an accommodation to overall ignorance, but this drab style was not inspirational, leaving the classrooms rather stale and stuffy. Not all of it was bad, though. I happily and gratefully acknowledge that it was through the creative devices of certain Sunday school teachers that I managed to learn the Lord's Prayer and the Nicene Creed in both Greek and English—line by line and by rote memorization. In a way, that appealed to my sense of competition, the teachers had a ladder in the classroom, and so, as you learned each line, your little paper-person would ascend rung by rung; when you reached the top, you were rewarded with a prize and your name listed on the board. A pretty effective incentive, I would say!

Follow the Bouncing Note

Sadly, I did not get very far with the services in church either. The Divine Liturgy felt important and mystical, but not at all compelling. The language issue was just so difficult to navigate, making it a headache to follow the service. So, I ended up studying the liturgy book, since it had little drawings and cartoons in the margins, for the purpose of explaining what was going on. Thank God for those illustrations, or I would have been totally blacked out. I am not saying that I was not aware of something spiritual and larger than myself occurring, but it was not clearly understood. No matter how bright a person is, it is simply unnatural to hear something in one language, and then try to follow along in another. This presented a real interior cacophony, the result of which was exhaustion and exasperation. Of course, I was grateful for the liturgical aides, as it helped me stay sane, but to be honest, what really got me interested in the church were musical tunes, both small and great. Never underestimate the power of a tiny tune. You never know what you may learn just from brief simple songs. Without these songs that were creatively employed, church would have been suffocating. The following, then, describes how these tunes—bits and bars of music—led me to worship more fully and to begin learning the old Byzantine music of the church.

There were two visible avenues that presented themselves for this learning to occur. The first avenue was conducted by Father Alexander Veronis, our parish priest and my spiritual father from this time and onwards through my life. Just after the Gospel, and just before the adult sermon, Father would address us during the children's sermonette. There we would sing campy Protestant songs, geared for little kids.

THE Fablehood TRILOGY

For instance, I grew up singing, "Jesus loves me, this I know…" and "Jesus, loves the little children," and other such fun songs. I knew that they had nothing to do with the Byzantine hymnology of the Divine Liturgy, and I knew that they were simple and not too heavy, but they had the advantage of being accessible and easy to grasp. Those Bambi-style tunes got me singing in the church, and I looked forward to this part of the service every week. Properly primed then, I was ready to listen to the brief children's message, which I greatly appreciated. I do not remember anything he said, but I certainly caught the energy and excitement, with which Father spoke during those times. They were all launched by little songs, led by the priest himself. He seemed to enjoy them and to take an interest in us, so I did too; I enjoyed the music, and my eyes and ears opened to hear the message. These teaching opportunities usually occurred right after the Gospel, but unfortunately, at least from my perspective, we were led downstairs to go to Sunday school. The children's portion was over, and now the adult sermon would ensue. But I never liked this departure from the church, as it felt very counter-intuitive; I mean, weren't we supposed to be in church and stay there? I was all primed and ready to go, and then the faucet was abruptly shut. We were carted off to the classrooms, and then the stifling boredom would seep into our brains beyond measure. I recall vowing to myself that someday I will not go return to Sunday school, but rather, stay for the adult Divine Liturgy to continue our worship.

The second avenue to participation, at least musically in the service, was when we would all be gathered together in the hall for a big music assembly.

Follow the Bouncing Note

One of the choir directors, Mr. Harry Nafliotis, would lead us to blackboards, upon which he had painstakingly written out the Greek hymns of the church in phonetic notation. This had to have taken an enormous amount of time, especially as he explained the meaning and place of the hymns during our worship. Then, with a pointer, he would bounce the tip of it over each note, singing very clearly and deliberately for us to follow. Hence, for instance, the hymn of Pentecost went like this, *"Ev-lo-gee-toss-ee Christ-ay-O, O Theos, Emon..."*, and it worked! I felt equipped and grateful for this man, and the labors he wrought. He taught both the how and why of the hymns; to sing them and to know where they apply. I have never forgotten him or Father Veronis for setting me on the path to love the Orthodox faith, one note at a time.

As a priest, and earlier as a youth director, I have used the same methods myself. I borrowed the phonetic translations, the method, and the assemblies to teach the same way. I even lifted the song books and approaches used at our church camp, Camp Nazareth, and adopted them for our own, But, because I have had limited success with these parish attempts at musical Christian education with students, I have instead transferred the concept to apply to the community as a whole. This means that we have adopted congregational singing as our musical worship motif, and I must say that I am very pleased with the results. The people are the choir; they do the singing. We designed a special book that puts everyone in the church "on the same page," and I must say that the results have been amazing.

In any event, these approaches are, in truth, all borrowed from my origins in the great church of

THE Fablehood TRILOGY

Lancaster. I have always felt that, if I could give even a quarter of what I received as a child, I would be the most effective teacher and priest I could possibly be. I was blessed, and I continue to share those blessings. Glory to God for all things!

CHIP 29: *Learning craves a moment. Never lose an opportunity to reach someone with a teachable moment. If necessary, use alternative methods, but do whatever it takes to reach them and teach them. Never, ever give up on anyone, especially where learning is concerned! Find the time, find the way, and find the key. Learning craves a moment.*

30

Kinder World

At some point, we are all compelled to cross the first big threshold in our lives, and yes, by this I mean, elementary school. These days, many children are ahead of the transitional game, as their parents have already introduced them to daycares and preschools, out of economic necessity. But back in the '60s the first public test for little kids was the transition from home to kindergarten. I remember feeling terrified, as my mom took me to the front door of the E. R. Martin Elementary School, and then down the left of the entrance to the kindergarten room. There we were met by a sweet teacher, who took my hand from my mother's hand and led me into the classroom. I was comforted to feel my teacher's apparent maternal presence.

For instance, I vividly recall crying terribly when certain songs would be played in our classroom. One of them "Go Tell Aunt Rhody," is an old Traditional song that some claim to be an English-language folk song of nineteenth-century American origin while others say that the Genevan philosopher Jean-

THE Fablehood TRILOGY

Jacques Rousseau had a hand in its making. It goes like this:

GO TELL AUNT RHODY

Go tell Aunt Rhody,
Go tell Aunt Rhody,
Go tell Aunt Rhody
The old gray goose is dead.

The one she's been saving,
The one she's been saving,
The one she's been saving
To make a feather bed.

The goslings are mourning,
The goslings are mourning,
The goslings are mourning,
Because their mother's dead.

The old gander's weeping,
The old gander's weeping,
The old gander's weeping,
Because his wife is dead.

She died in the mill pond,
She died in the mill pond,
She died in the mill pond
From standing on her head.

Go tell Aunt Rhody,
Go tell Aunt Rhody,
Go tell Aunt Rhody
The old gray goose is dead.

Kinder World

I wondered, "Why all this death and darkness? Why sing about depressing topics?" So, I reached my arms around her waist and clutched her dress with my tears and was soon comforted.

Another song that used to break me up and make me go in circles was "Both Sides Now" performed by Joni Mitchell. The lyrics would take me into a tailspin. It sang of looking at life from both sides now and that "it's life's illusions" that the singer recalls, but really she doesn't "know life at all."

I had no idea what this song was about, and I am not sure I even know now, but our teacher loved it. I clutched at her skirt for this one too, and for any of the Simon and Garfunkel songs she sang. Thank God for her kindness to me!

It was not easy to break into a new and public world. I recall the scene as if it were yesterday. With her hand on my shoulder, she introduced me to the class. As I looked out on the assembly of kids staring back at me, I felt as though I had just landed on another planet. They were all white kids, American kids, who had no idea about Greece or olive oil or feta cheese. These were all country kids, with names like Sue, Robert, Kevin, and so forth. They all looked as if they came from the same farm. How could I possibly fit in here, I thought to myself. I am the only "non-white" person here! If I could have turned and run back, I would have. My eyes began to moisten and my lips tremored.

But just then, a sunny blond boy came up to our teacher and spoke in the politest terms I had ever heard in my brief life, saying, "Pardon me. May I please get up for a drink of water?" And, noticing me, he said, "Is he a new boy in the class?" The teacher, of course, nodded approval to both questions, and with a smile and a confident handshake, he turned directly to me and introduced himself: "Hi, I'm Hank Summy! Where are you sitting?" The teacher escorted me to my desk, and I was situated very quickly. When he came back from his sip, Hank continued to smile and continued to be pleasant to me. In fact, he was unbelievably polite with everyone. I had never heard anyone speak so properly before, or experienced such gentlemanly behavior anywhere, not in my home or even at church. His exhibition of such civility was quite striking, but most importantly, it was comforting. He was the real deal, no pretending or faking with Hank. He was kind and solicitous to everyone, and not just the teacher, but to everyone. He was not an idle flatterer or a braggart, a brown-nose, or anything fake. I had never heard anyone say "thank you," "may I", "pardon me," "yes ma'am," and "excuse me" as much in all my life, but here he was, day in and day out with the same well-heeled character. And from the beginning, he welcomed me.

I never forgot Hank's kindness to me. But I was no one special. He was like that with everyone. Some folks are just first class. Indeed, all the boys felt comfortable with him, as he was easy to get along and to play with. I do not know what the girls thought of him back then, but there was no mistaking their notice of him in the coming years. I would go on to junior high and senior high school with Hank, and graduate with him. He was adored, and annually elected to every homecoming court, and deservedly so. I recall one time, many years after we had graduated, I went to visit my parents in Lancaster. Dad was at his barbershop, and out of the door came a tall, dusty-blond haired, man, with a crew cut and a firm military bearing. My dad said to me, "You know Mr. Summy, don't you?" Before I could reply, Mr. Summy (the father of my classmate, Hank) reached out his hand to me, and said, "I want you to know that your dad is true blue, a really good man, and I feel privileged and honored to have my hair cut here. You are a very blessed, young man!" As my dad blushed with the kind sincerity of this gentleman, I could hear myself say in reply, "Yes sir! Thank you! A pleasure to meet you!" And indeed it was. I felt the circle of life close perfectly upon me at that moment, What was true at kindergarten, and on through the years, apparently was always true. Now, I knew why.

CHIP 30: *A word of kindness never fails. Class begets class, and barbarism begets barbarism. We become who we model. Or, quite simply, "The apple does not fall too far from the tree." I have been blessed to benefit from good people, folks who lifted me up by their simple civility, a disposition not accidental but learned in the home and shared abroad. Thank God for such social smoothing. My life has been the better for simple words and actions. A word of kindness never fails.*

31

Recess Warfare

The door to freedom was at the back of the room, where it freed us to the playground outside. The immediate area consisted of a collection of four square courts, hopscotch areas, and assorted jungle gyms. There were all kinds of opportunities to burn off some of your energy. But beyond those macadam-surfaced exercises, and seeming to roll on forever, were fields upon fields. A number of us boys would go out as far as we could, and there we would gather for our own sport. Someone would bring a football, or any kind of ball, and our aim was to play as wildly as we could. Our game of choice was something called "Smear the Queer," admittedly a title that would certainly not fly today, not politically correct enough, but at the time, we never conceived the name or ever meant it as a political or gender statement. After all, we were barely conscious that we had a gender, or even what that was. We were only concerned about one thing at recess, and that was to romp along in our rough and tumble. The object of our "game" was to cream the guy with the ball, to knock him silly, and

Recess Warfare

to get the ball and run until you got smeared. That was the mechanics of our sophisticated game. And I thought I was pretty good at it.

Well, that was until this one boy came along. Oh, I was fast and nimble, light on my feet, and I would often breeze past my munchkin foes, and when I would finally get tackled, I would lower my shoulder and drive my body firmly into my tackler, just to teach him a lesson. This punishing, brutal assault was generally most effective, until I drove my shoulder into a waiting Kam Kettering. Yes, that was his name, odd, but he should have been named "Ram Battering" instead, because when I attempted to pound myself into him, he seemed to have built a brick wall in front of himself to greet me. Boom! He was "the immovable object," whom upon "meeting" greeted me with a bounce into a new reality. Kam was not big or bursting with muscles, but he had that innate country-boy strength, that was not contrived or molded, but learned from his home. I imagined that he must have baled hay or wrestled with farm animals, because he was truly a force of nature. Consequently, Kam had no trouble at all separating me from the pigskin I thought that I could keep snugly in my possession.

And then, after the ball was aggressively ripped from my penmanship paws, Kam started to run. I recall distinctly that he took off for the cornfields at the border of our school property, an area that we were utterly forbidden to go near. Kam tore toward "*terra incognita*," and we all had it in our minds to stop him. Still confident enough in my "Speedy Gonzales" pace, I caught up to him and dove at his waist to bring him down, whereupon I found that I was

THE Fablehood TRILOGY

being carried like a loaf of bread toward the boundary. Then other boys joined in, all of us grabbing on to him, and one upon another, he carried us along, like a massive bull tossing away his skinny tormentors. Not a single one of us dared to wrap him up around the legs, to put the full tackle upon him, lest we risk getting our teeth displaced by the pounding of his pumping pistons. Dragged about as if we were tied to a team of horses, we were led on an unscheduled tour of the school lands. We were all in disbelief, at least I was. Finally, and mercifully, and not because we slowed him down, Kam stopped right before the cornfields ahead of us, and we all collapsed around him. Of course, he still retained the ball, since no one could pry it out of his hands, which he tossed into the air for someone else to retrieve. He laughed and smiled graciously, and with his muscular hand, helped me up from the ground. I stood beside him and just shook my head, knowing that my own boundaries were now clearly indicated. He was a force of nature! Of course, we would continue to play our little game, as long as Kam allowed us.

CHIP 31: *All DNAs are not created equal. Thankfully, we are all different. There is always someone who is going to be better than you are and someone who is worse than you are. That is okay. We are all designed by a Divine Artist. Accept who you are. All DNAs are not created equal. Thankfully, we are all different.*

32

Bus Stop Buddies

The bus stop had a life of its own. Every morning I would go out the front door to my bus stop, which was conveniently located in front of our neighbor's house on the right. As I left my house, I could see Dad sitting in a cloud of foul cigarette smoke and drinking jet black coffee. While standing patiently at the end of their driveway waiting for my fellow bus mates, I would create a fog with my breath in the cold morning air. Meanwhile, I would hear the "Whoo-hoo, hoo-hoo" of a mourning dove, greeting his bride with some early morning songs and hopes. I recall the peacefulness of those idylls in the first part of the day. It was so refreshing and liberating for my soul.

And yet, when my friends joined me at the bus stop, my heart leapt at the opportunity of their company. Their names and faces are still fresh in my mind: Craig Hoin, Joel DeCamp, and then, later we were joined on the bus by Duane Good, Kam Kettering, Jeff Lepore, David Longenecker, and who knows who else. Duane was always fun to sit next

THE Fablehood TRILOGY

to, as he knew everything about the Chicago Bears and a player called Dick Butkus. Jeff would describe his latest scientific and photography projects, with plenty of weird experimentation and advancement in science that was way beyond our age. (He eventually went on to become a world-class photographer.) We all had a marvelous time on our way to school. We would banter about anything and joke easily and freely, as we enjoyed the freedom to relax and revel in the moment.

And really, that was the point—to enjoy the bus stop and the ride that followed, as some of the best moments of my childhood. The time seemed to fly as we began our day together. Indeed, how wonderful it was to start the day with laughter. I knew, even then, that these times were passing quickly, and that it was critical to enjoy them in a manner that was fulfilling. After all, we each knew that we would soon move on to our separate places and be replaced with new friends. that life would be changing very fast from here on out. Soon, everything would change. And so it did. Junior high school was looming, in fact, some of the kids had already gone elsewhere, and our bus stop reverie would come to an end. Later, in my adult years, I even looked up a couple of our crew, and they too remembered the wonderful times we had. I have had many "bus stop" moments in my life, but these set the journey for the rest of my life.

CHIP 32: *There is nothing random about the "people along the way." Think of all the "bus stops" in life, where you get to meet folks who fill up your time with color and commen-*

Bus Stop Buddies

tary. They are gifts from God for a passing time, and then you move on. God puts individuals in our lives to enlarge us and to benefit others. For kindness among so-called "strangers" is heavenly hospitality. So, seize the moments, and the personalities in them, while you can. Life is full of people of joy, even in their sadness, if only we would wake up and respond to them. Embrace the bus stops. Just remember: There is nothing random about the "people along the way."

33

Hangers On

In my closet, there are hangers that are never used for anything at all. Set off in a corner that only I can see, they just hang there as an artifact of the distant hands that created them. For these are not just your run-of-the-mill clothing hangers. Rather, they are works of art produced by tiny young hands, the hands of the little girls I had a crush on in the third grade. Taking various colors of yarn, Abby and Daria would weave and wind their cotton spools in creative patterns on metal hangers to alter their appearance completely to create "art." Now, how did I come into the possession of such individualized forms of tapestry? I don't really know, but what I do know is what I can remember.

    I certainly remember that I liked these girls, and, to my great surprise, they liked me too, though I do not think it was at the same time. I recall another girl with whom I had this same mutual infatuation. Each of them was attractive in her own way, and I was unashamedly smitten with the love bug. Of course, the reader may be excused for thinking that these

Hangers On

whole amorous interests are ridiculous or the stuff of an over-eager imagination. But I recall these small flames as if I had just seen them yesterday. Allow me to introduce them to you.

Abby Shear was a raven-haired beauty with charcoal dark eyes and an olive complexion. She had the classic features of an Aegean goddess, adorned with youthful freckles, and hair that was full and thick. There was a coarseness to her hair, as if her head were topped in ebony lamb's wool, but without the curls, just long and brushed out to frame her face. I could not take my eyes off her, and I am certain that she knew it, as she would sometimes flash her almond shaped eyes back at me. She was beautiful, but approachable; smart, without being overbearing; and I was thoroughly smitten. At some point, she broke my heart because she told me that we could never be together forever, since she was Jewish, and I was Christian. Nevertheless, we remained close, and I knew then that we both loved each other as much as the limitations of our circumstances would allow. *To express her affection, and as a parting artifact of our brief time together, she gave me one of the decorated hangers. And I have held on to it ever since. After that grade, somewhere in the world of E. R. Martin Elementary School, we left our love behind.*

Then there was Daria Hubiak. She was someone I found immensely magnetic, though not for the same kind of striking beauty as Abby. Her appeal was her intelligence and her exotic Russian background, which seemed to radiate from her. I had a definite advantage with Daria, in that we did not have to explain each other's faith and culture. We were both Orthodox, and that was a connection that was extraordinarily powerful, even at that early time of my life. Steeped in the faith, Daria could sing the melodious hymns of her Russian Orthodox Church, which she learned from her father who was a cantor. Moreover, she was sharp and focused, like a mother who is in control of the whole family home. Indeed, Daria was maternal, which seems like an odd thing to say for someone in grade school, but she seemed to have an older soul, with a wisdom that reminded me of, well, my mother. I was smitten with Daria, but also terrified of her. This is the kind of girl you marry, someone who would have been the ideal person to have in my life as a serious Orthodox and as a priest. I know that she felt the same way, but with the limitations of life, one could not be tied down from such a young age. Daria was the "right girl" but at the wrong time. Besides, she ended up moving near Harrisburg, so we had to get used to the idea of being apart forever. *To express her affection, and as a parting artifact of our brief time together, she gave me another of the decorated hangers. And I have held on to it ever since. After that grade, somewhere in the world of E. R. Martin Elementary School, we left our love behind.*

    Years would pass, at least forty or so, and I was assigned as an assistant priest at the Greek Orthodox Church in Richmond, Virginia. It was there that I met a parishioner, Athena Conte, who mentioned that when she lived in Wisconsin, she had an old friend, who relayed that she once had a boyfriend in elementary school. The friend wondered whatever happened to her old beau, hearing that he had become a priest. Athena seemed to recall that my name was mentioned, but she was not sure, so I asked her what her friend's name was. She replied, "Daria." I was

Hangers On

dumbfounded, but thankful for the amazing circles of life. As life would have it, I would later meet Daria a couple of times at weddings and events associated with Athena, and when I saw her, we had the rarest of connections. Though she was married, just as I was, we each paused—just long enough and for the slightest moment—and remembered.

CHIP 33: *Love, once experienced, never dies. Even if the exchange of affection happened in early springs of youth or in autumnal or wintry climes, Love endures and is eternal. We are formed by gestures of love, sustained in their ability to lift us out of the moment and into eternal remembrance. The heart is a muscle that never forgets, especially when it has received gifts from another. Love, once experienced, never dies.*

34

Banana Splits

There is no greater freedom for a child than a bicycle, and no set of wheels quite as hip as the "banana seat" version. Take some playing cards and some clothespins, and by attaching them to the frame and their interference with the winding wheels, you can instantly create a motorized whir to your bike. You can also take a flag, attach it to a flexible pole secured to the rear of the seat, and suddenly everyone knows how cool you are. And, when you are riding, you can lean back and "pop a wheelie," meaning that you lift the front end of the bike up, and ride only on the back wheel. You could ride all kinds of ways: by sitting, standing, by yourself, or with someone on the seat with you. Life in the banana seat sure was wonderful! I felt like a noble knight on two wheels.

And, most importantly for me was the freedom to go anywhere at any time I wanted. I could "take a spin" and sidle up to any home I wanted or even make a surprise visit to unsuspecting friends. And when it was time to leave, I could just jump on my cool bike and ride home. Or, I could spy and dart here and there whenever I wanted to observe someone, but then hide. Freedom, thy name is "Banana Seat Bike."

In the afternoons after school, I would hop on the bike and go and see my friends, usually in "Quaker Hills," the Brady Bunch-looking neighborhood across from us on the Millersville Pike. Houses on our street were hard to get to because of the major road we lived on, but also because they were so set back and separated by huge properties. Indeed, our home was situated on a prime two acre lot, set back from the Millersville Pike by a sprawling field of green. The house was a Cape Cod style, lengthy, over 90 feet. Capped with slate roofs and bordered all around with flagstones, the elongated brick house was painted white, with blue shutters around the windows. Setting the perimeter of the yard were split-rail fences, reminiscent of horse farms. I could go in any direction.

If I went into Quaker Hills, a group of us would gather at Joel DeCamp's house and sit on wide comfy sofas to watch "Ultra Man," "The Banana Splits," or "Speed Racer," before going outside to play our brutal expression of tackle football in the backyard. When one of their parents told us it was dinner time, I would head back home. But not always. Sometimes, I would ride a little further and visit a quarry nearby, where I, and whoever wished to join me, would throw rocks to hear the splashes and echoes far below. On my way home, I would make sure to glide by the house where Terry, a fetching short-haired girl lived, and we would stop and talk from our bikes. I never went into her house or saw her parents. I just loved that I could stop by and see her. I guess you could say that I had a crush on her, and that qualified

THE Fablehood TRILOGY

her as a girlfriend, but all I could ever do was stop by and then leave, and that was enough. There were other homes that I could deign to visit, but then it was great to say, "Well, gotta go now!" And I would be off and back home by nightfall, without anyone asking where I was or what I was doing. Or, if they did, I would say, "Just out and around, you know." And that would be enough. My parents had incredible trust. What freedom!

If I went in the direction of my own home, the boys from Quaker Hills would come up to my little world, and we would ride our bikes into the corn fields around my house. If we could knock down enough cornstalks, then we could say that we made our fort, and throw corn at each other, as if we were at war. At the other end of the cornfield, there was a barn with an old silo. We would make our way into the barn and jump on bales of hay from the loft above. What a great life you can have from a bike! A pond lay beyond the barn, and we could watch fish and see if we could hit them with acorns. I must say that the only problem I had with the farm were the horses, which were enormous and terrifying to me, so I was sure to avoid them. (To this day, I still shudder when I see a large horse, so I guess I have a case of "hippophobia!") If we were lucky, we would find purple berries and crush them into our hands to make Indian war paint, as we imagined ourselves in an untamed wilderness—when, naturally, we were the only untamed ones. Returning by a dirt road to my house, we would hide behind bushes, and with an arsenal of freshly picked rocks, we would toss them at the traffic going by on the Millersville Pike. Then we would watch as folks would slow down and get irate.

Yes, all of this was incredibly stupid, but the freedom of these adventures was incredibly intoxicating.

On occasion, we would even go to the white-picketed houses alongside the Pike, where the rich kids lived, and play in well-paneled rooms with electric race cars and stuffed animals. We would leave at "homework time," and venture back to the fields, where we could hit rocks with sticks or light fires in the big trash barrel. Other times, we would ride down to fishing holes, shopping centers, golf courses, or schools, or wherever our wheels would take us. We had the beautiful freedom to do as we pleased, to go where we pleased, and to stay out as long as we pleased, that is, as long as we were home by dinner.

CHIP 34: *Childhood is a necessary playground for life. We are blessed when we have ample time and freedom to play; we are hindered and hampered when we don't. For a healthy maturity is forged in pretend land and wounded by too much reality. Thank God when we are blessed with backyards of friendship, places simply to be and to let go, where adventures are just a spin or two away, and there is immeasurable time to imagine. Childhood is a necessary playground for life.*

35

Faculty Faculties

My first love in school was science. Give me a couple of batteries and some wiring, and I could flip the electromagnetic switch. Electricity by friction, by battery, by lightning all fascinated me. But what was most delightful was the study of the animal kingdoms. I had no better laboratory than by the window of my room where I would use the fresh natural sunlight to illuminate my drawings of birds, squirrels, trees, and whatever I could see outside. I would make the sketch and then fill in the colors of robins, blue jays, chipmunks, acorns, or what have you, with colored pencils. I am not sure what teacher to applaud for this interest in science, but I think it might have been Mrs. Hill in third grade.

My earlier teachers were very caring and attentive, but Mrs. Hill challenged us and opened our minds. We were constantly writing reports, for which my dad would drive me and George to the library. There I would look up the theme we were studying and then copy whole passages from the encyclopedia, while changing one or two words or lines to make the work seem like it was mine. It was pathetic, dishonorable, and the wrong thing to do, but it was effective! I knew it was deceitful, but the shortcuts in completing the assigned reports soothed my impatient and anxious mind. Better yet, I truly experienced true learning that made me hunger for more knowledge. Dad had whole sets of encyclopedias, atlases, history books, books on art, philosophy, sailing, drawing, subjects that would intoxicate my mind with the inebriate of education. Increasingly, I found myself immersed in the pages of a book.

In our classroom, I recall that we had to complete "packets," reams of materials, separated by sections and having little tests at the end. I devoured these with gusto and kept pushing to complete the packets in all my studies: mathematics, social studies, history, English, but especially science. My learning was compulsive and obsessive, but among all the subjects, I enjoyed science more than the others because it represented the discovery of pure knowledge. I had no ambition toward any scientific field with these studies; I just enjoyed the thrill of learning something new every day. My mind had been awakened.

I found myself racing forward with an ever-expanding understanding of the world, and feeling very proud and confident with myself. But I came to understand that there is a huge difference between knowledge, such as with "book smart," and knowing how to get along with others, better termed as "social intelligence," or quite simply, "common sense." It became apparent that the more I learned from studying, the less I exercised any other form of intelligence, and that would soon lead to trouble. A great gulf was

THE Fablehood TRILOGY

developing between what I knew intellectually and how I related to others.

During the fifth grade, I would learn my lesson in a severe way. I behaved horribly. Here was the situation. I was in a foul mood because some kids, and in particular, Brad, whose last name I will keep to myself, were making fun of me before I boarded the school bus to go home. I was certainly used to being teased. Sometimes, I was deliberately demeaned when some boys would call me "Monk," short for "Monkey-Face," as they would walk around in gorilla-styled steps, to impersonate my way of moving. "Four-eyes" was another not so flattering moniker that was hurled at me, but this and other names I generally allowed to roll off my back. But there was something very annoying about this boy, Brad, who was snarly, sharp-tongued, and who possessed an outright mean streak that easily got under my skin. So, as I got into the bus, I decided I would get even with him. While he remained by the sidewalk, I got to my seat, pulled the window down, and called him over as if to say something to him. When he came close to the window, he lifted up his freckled obnoxious face, and I doused him with a huge wad of spit. As he screamed in disgust, I quickly closed the window and slunk back in the seat so as not to see him railing at the bus. But that is not the end of the story. My poor judgment would now get much worse. Ugh!

I was still in a foul mood because, while I was happy to spit on Brad—it really felt liberating—I knew it was beneath me, and I felt horrible about myself. What an ugly thing to do, and I should have been the better person. But I was angry at being treated like an exploding pus-filled zit, and so I wasn't done, not yet, not even close. I still had other scores to settle.

Another bratty kid, Lisa, sat in front of me on the bus. She was a girl who never had a kind thing to say to me. And now, there she was, right in front of me, like a gift to offer to my bruised self. Her hair, red and wild, was directly in front of me like a huge pumpkin waiting to be smashed. Full of whatever concoction of piss and vinegar that would cause a person to lose his good judgment, I noticed a whole tangle of gum and cigarette butts on the floor of the bus. It would not take much, I mused to myself, to gather the half-chewed, half darkened gum from the floor, and mix in about ten or twenty half-spent Camels to create a messy goo, perfect to drop into Lisa's hair. It would be so easy. How could I not do it? So, having made my grimy sachet of dust and detritus, I seized the disgusting bundle, lifted my hands above her head, and gave Lisa a dowsing she would never forget. Scooping a little bit at a time, so she wouldn't notice, and then more and more, I was able to get the whole mass of scummy trash onto her straggly hairy head, so that when Lisa finally lifted her hands to see what was going on with her hair, she ended up mixing the insulting "napalm" deeper into her scalp. She ended up screaming and leaning back over the seat, and accusing me of doing such a dastardly deed. With the incriminating grey and black soot of the cigarettes still on my fingers, I lied and denied any culpability in the matter. I mentioned that there must be spiders on the bus, or something like that. Completely humiliated, she burst into tears, while I just shrunk in my seat until it all passed. It should have been so easy and rewarding, but alas, revenge was just not as sweet as I thought it would be. Finally, I could breathe a bit when she got off the bus in tears, assuring me that I would pay.

And pay I did. Next time we were back in Mr. K's fifth grade classroom, Lisa showed up with her hair trimmed to a buzz cut, as if she had just gone through chemotherapy. She looked horrible. Her eyes were swollen from crying, and as she stood there in front of me and the whole class, I could see that she was just a little girl, a wounded and pathetic soul, and that my actions were beyond mean. They were stupid and did not rise to the dignity of any justification. She did not deserve this kind of treatment, no matter how she treated me before. I had violated her in a way that was simply galling, so that when Mr. K. asked if I had done this heinous act, I readily admitted it. "What were you thinking?" he asked me. I had no answer. The truth, of course, is that I had stopped thinking. I went temporarily insane, and this was the result. In any event, I felt terrible for her, and I was open to whatever punishment would come my way. I had never been paddled before (at least not that I could remember, not at home or school or anywhere). So when he rolled up his sleeves and pulled out the paddle, I was more shocked than pained. He took me out to the hallway, while another teacher watched the class, and then this well-built man, with his rolled up white sleeved shirt and artful tie held firm by a clip, his lips tight beneath his black mustache, took hold of the paddle and smacked me good and hard. I leaned against the wall with my hands, and endured the punishment, which hurt plenty enough, physically at least, but not enough to hurt me, though I knew that if he wanted to, Mr. K. could have made it much more intense. What hurt me more was the inner humiliation and embarrassment and shame I felt. I had never been thwacked before, and I was not proud of this moment, not one bit! To retain some dignity, I held back my tears, lowered my head, and quietly returned to my seat. Nothing more was said.

I ended up getting along very well with Mr. K., as I loved having a male teacher in elementary school. I completely supported what he had to do, and we became fairly close afterward. I never had anything more to do with Lisa, and Brad (my spit victim) left me alone forever, thank God. That was, quite obviously, the low point of my grade school experiences, but I was focused from there on out. The next year, in sixth grade, I felt liberated and, dare I say, confident—confident enough to take a lead role in Mrs. Rotz's performance of "Julius Caesar." Since I was one of the few kids to volunteer to act in a play by William Shakespeare, and since I had the confidence of Mrs. Rotz, I felt compelled to do the part. I can still taste the excitement of being on stage and the weight of responsibility to deliver my lines, which I muddled my way through. The relief when it was all over was so freeing that I felt as if I had just graduated from some challenging university.

In my heart, I knew that I would recall these low and high moments for the rest of my life. I still feel awful for my terrible actions with Brad and Lisa. Oh regret, thy name is "experience." And as for my encounter with Mr. Shakespeare and his wordy plays, I came to realize that the stage was increasingly my friend. No regrets there, except that I wish that I had done more acting during those years.

THE Fablehood TRILOGY

CHIP 35: *Act your best at each stage in life. It has been said by a certain famous bard that "all of life's a stage," lived one act at a time. Truer words could not have been said, for whatever the stage we are upon in our personal theater, we would be wise to follow some good advice—-and that is to be the very height of ourselves each time. Life is a revolving stage, and we are given a cameo role upon cameo role, testing us, challenging us, imploring us to be the utmost that we can be. Regret is not an illusion; it is itself regrettable. Therefore, let us choose wisely whenever we can. Act your best at each stage in life.*

36
Greek School Dropout

"Regret is an adult preoccupation," quipped Dr. Wooby, one of my professors at Millersville University. And so it is, in my autumn years, that I manifest my former teacher's sentiments. I do indeed feel regret, and this "adult preoccupation" centers on not learning the Greek language, a tongue that was offered to me repeatedly. But I would prove to be foolishly bull-headed in my determination not to submit to the pressures of Hellenization. Even as a child, I was sensitive to how I was perceived and labeled. To those from Greece, I was an *"Americanaki,"* and to the Americans, I was a "Greek boy." Neither tag worked for me, as I was not sure who or what I was. I lived my days straddling a hyphen identity.

The world at home was decidedly Greek, but the rest of the world in which I lived was "American." I understood, or at least believed, as did many others in my situation, that to be accepted into the larger society, you had to walk, talk, and behave as an American. I had to fit in, so I thought, or I would become a nobody. That meant eschewing the demands and

THE *Fablehood* TRILOGY

prerogatives of being Greek, however it presented itself. That meant a "heels dug in no" to all phases of the culture that was different from the supreme majority—a rejection of the language, customs, and traditions of my people. I would keep the Greek food, but not much else. I drew a line at learning the language, or rather, being forced to learn the language. It seemed so unfair. My peers at school did not have to do any such thing, why should I? It was the forced aspect of the matter that felt so suffocating and was the fuel to my rebellious spirit. By the way, others of my Greek American generation cut out even more of our Greek heritage than I did. Some even went so far as abandoning the Church and its traditions, which for me was simply going too far. But the pressure to be "Greek" in America had a terrible chokehold over me, and regrettably, cut off oxygen to my brain and my wiser senses.

Of course, my mother tried to convince and even teach me in an easy and non-threatening manner, but I would have none of it. She would, for instance, say, "*Dos mou ena poteeree nero*," for "Give me a glass of water," and other phrases like that. I learned them well enough, but there was a limitation in the world to "kitchen-Greek," so I soon abandoned it, though I certainly remember all the words for pots and pans and such! Then there were the attempts to go to "Greek School," classes that were held at the church and usually taught by home-spun olive-oiled drill instructors of the maternal persuasion. They certainly meant well, but I just found the whole experience of reciting poems and learning verb conjugations and declensions of nouns insufferably boring. The whole thing felt like a denial of my reality, which was that I

Greek School Dropout

lived in America, not in some village in the Peloponnisos. I felt so guilty, as well, since Mom wanted me to be fluent in Greek and appreciative of her culture, which of course was a reasonable request. But all I could do was rebel and disappoint her. She cajoled, persuaded, reasoned, simplified, and encouraged me to learn, but I refused. I stood my ground like a mule at the edge of a cliff. In her prudent wisdom, she pushed me to a point, but then would not mandate or demand. To Mom's credit, and to her fault, she respected my freedom. The "last straw" occurred one day when Mom got into the car and told me to hop in, which I refused to do. I knew she was going to the church to teach Greek, and I would have none of it. My mature response was to climb up a tree, and hope that she would not see me. Of course, she did see me and duly informed me that I could stay up there all night as far as she was concerned. That was the day when I became a Greek School dropout, a decision I would rue for decades. Oh, such regrettable stubbornness!

I should add, however, that our general practice at home was that Mom would talk to me in Greek, and I would answer in English, a practice that has been representative of my relationship with the language ever since. To wit, I understand Greek fully, but lack a certain level of confidence to converse in it. Karen has noticed that when I am among Greeks, and particularly when we would go back to Lancaster, that I would become "more Greek," and talk more freely. In any event, later in life, when I got more serious about learning Greek in the seminary, and less hung up on identity issues—as real and relevant as they were—I gained some ground in the world of grammar and

THE Fablehood TRILOGY

phrasing. I am supremely grateful for the great professors who helped me, but I must say, quite honestly, that I have never been fully Hellenized. Ugh! How shortsighted I was. Greek would have been a great tool for ministry, and in general, but I was resolved to bury my head so far into the sand that only my rear end would show. How foolish! As good old Dr. Wooby would famously say, "Regret is an adult preoccupation." It certainly is.

CHIP 36: *An opportunity lost is a regret forever. Thus, it is wise to avoid climbing trees when a revving auto is available to take you further along in your journey. In fact, you may gain knowledge or a valuable lifelong skill by welcoming the opportunity when it is granted to you. The truth is that a door does not stay open forever, and once closed, is difficult to open again. Walk through the door of learning while it is offered or suffer its woeful closure. An opportunity lost is a regret forever.*

37

Button-Down Shirts

Long sleeve shirts, especially white button-down ones, were once essential to my attire. Short sleeves exposed my arms, and since I did not feel particularly muscular, I did not wear them. I was a kid who was as skinny as a rail and terribly self-conscious, so I would make sure that the shirts were buttoned all the way to the top, and often, I would don a tie, just to look formal and respectable. The label, "dweeb" or "nerd," would apply perfectly.

Not only my shirt, but my hair was also challenged. When it was not cut short to the scalp, my hair would grow out wildly and curly. If I had let it run rampant, my head would have been topped with a wavy thick mop of coarse undulating rags. The curls were so arched and mountainous that they looked as if a sculptor had freed them from clay. Not wanting to have my hair look too dramatic or, God forbid, attractive, I would take a bristly brush and stroke out my curls toward my eyes, so that the hair on my head would wave upward, just before my eyebrows. I looked like someone had built a mini ski jump at my

THE Fablehood TRILOGY

forehead. My brother, George, would talk pointedly to me, "Good Lord! You look horrible. Why don't you do something with yourself? If you want, you can go to my stylist, but please, don't go to Dad. He'll make things worse. Good God, do something about your style!" Well, I did. I chose to have no style at all.

Oh, and, lest I forget, pants were also an issue. The pants could certainly not be too stylish or attractive. Oh no! They had to be straight but could not be too well cut or tailored. The point of this "style," was not to have a style at all or draw attention to myself. In psychobabble terms, "I did not feel good about myself," so I adopted the diminished demeanor of a dour dork. Or, so I thought.

The adults in my world seemed to find my look somewhat charming, as if I were someone who did not need to be affirmed by external praise. They did not see, or they were too polite to observe, an insecure and terrified child. Instead, perhaps because I always spoke to them with deference and in a mannerly way, they thought I was someone who was more mature, someone unlike the other kids, who were swayed by fashions and trends and the beat of our era. I was a throwback to an earlier time when kids were more respectful, whereas they were good eggs and swell fellas. I was "serious," whereas my peers were frivolous. I had "depth of thought," whereas others were shallow. I stood for being a selfless, non-materialistic, and humble "Christian," whereas others ignored religion entirely. I read and studied and hung the star of academic virtue about my neck, while those other shiftless dolts—my peers—would sit in less ponderous chairs. Lord, almighty, I was really something! Oh, I was so "religious," well-tucked, manicured, and

Button-Down Shirts

clean, but inside, I lacked the passion to offer someone true love. I was observant, and even knowledgeable, but it was all crisp folds and buttoned-down. Even I believed it. I did not realize that I was living in a world of pretend.

The truth, of course, is that I just wanted to be approved of, liked, affirmed, applauded, admired. Was that asking for too much? Playing the nerdy intellectual card, which, by the way, my siblings saw right through, I could present the answer that would give the adults in my world the best impression of me. Hence, when they would look me over, as adults seemed to practice so well, they would inevitably ask, "Oh, Yiannaki! (Johnny)," What do you think you will be when you grow up?" This was a question, by the way, that I realized had less to do with me than with my parents, as if they, and not I, were being tested. The nosy grown-ups would, I imagined, talk excitedly to one another about what his or her son or daughter will do to "make a living" in their lives. They would compare these parallel ambitions and either make nods of approval or not. Well, since I did not want to see my parents unduly criticized or harshly judged because of me—in other words, I did not want to embarrass them—when the question would inevitably be asked of me, I would blurt out as loudly as I could, "I want to be a doctor." Of course, I had no interest in becoming a doctor, not in the least. It just sounded good. I could see that "becoming a doctor" seemed to elicit the most approving smiles, so I stuck with the lie as best as I could. Why disappoint people, I reasoned? Furthermore, I felt proud to say it, as if saying it would fulfill every hope and praise my parents could expect. So, I kept that little fib well-hidden

THE Fablehood TRILOGY

for as long as possible. It wouldn't hurt if, even in the meantime, I could practice the part, properly costumed by a bleachy long-sleeved button-down shirt.

CHIP 37: *Never pretend to be someone you are not. There is no shortage of pressures in life to please others, particularly when trying to satisfy those who share your genetic code. These folks who orbit our lives certainly mean well, but their intentions can unintentionally become traps and snares, where one can easily lose an irreplaceable paw. The truth is that our pawprints are ours and ours alone. And so, do be most grateful for loving counsel, but be wary of it when it blurs your own footprint. Fight ferociously to take your own steps in life. Never pretend to be someone you are not.*

38

Altar Boy Antics

The sacred area around altar of the church is referred to as "the sanctuary" or, in Greek, the "*iero*." The name indicates a holy place, after the prototype found in Solomon's Temple, the "Holy of Holies." Such an environment was to be accorded the highest respect, or even further, profound reverence. Reverence was the attitude appropriate for the holy altar, a place set apart for the majesty of God, the presence of the Almighty, an area where God "resides," a place where God is due proper awe and utter silence.

Unless, of course, you served at the altar as an "altar boy," then you could desecrate the solemn ground any time you wanted. We "served" at the altar—in other words, we gave our time and attention to the smooth running of the service, especially when the worship offered the "holy mysteries," that is, the "sacred Body and Blood of the Lord." We really thought of ourselves as integral to the entire ceremony and necessary components of the liturgical actions that were being offered, since we, and we

THE Fablehood TRILOGY

alone, provided the bread and the wine and water and even the smoke of heaven-bound incense to make it all happen. Naturally, if we were not there, how could the service continue? We were right up there, up front, to be up staged, if that were ever to occur, only by the priest himself. You might say that we considered ourselves to be quite the "Big Deal," and yet clearly were not. We were just kids. Although we were clad in handsome robes and carried beeswax candles and silver processional fans, we were more "boys" than "altar." Our "job," if you can believe it, was for us to represent the angelic powers, ceaselessly worshiping God around his heavenly throne for eternity. Angels indeed! Angels, perhaps—but more like "fallen angels."

My Lord, we were anything but angelic. Demonic would be a better adjective to describe us. Oh, you are wondering, who is the "us"? We were the sons who were volunteered by their parents, or sometimes by the priest, to offer their time of service at the holy altar. In truth, all the boys in the church were offered this sacred opportunity, but only those who accepted the role could be considered part of the crew. Each week featured a different crew of boys, usually about seven or eight kids, the chief of whom was called the "Captain." He was the alpha, the "big cheese," the one who made all the decisions about who would carry what item out in a procession, or who would bring the water or the bread for Father, or hold the cloth for holy communion, or whatever. The Captain assigned the duties, arranged the order, and kept discipline while everyone else was expected to do their duties peacefully and obediently. He made sure that all the boys were dressed appropriately in their robes, and that they hung them properly after the service. Moreover, the Captain was generally the only one who could speak to the priest. He waited for orders from the Man at the front of the table, the holy altar, and then executed them down the line of willing soldiers. We were supposed to work with the efficiency of a well-trained and disciplined platoon—except we didn't.

We certainly did not work as a mature team because the problem with being boys and only having half our brain cells intact, was that we were still just boys. Angels were mature, elegant, beautiful creatures, aloft on gossamer wings and alight with the fire of divinity. We were "boys"—smelly, rude, unkempt, irascible rodents—each of whom thought of himself as the alpha, the rightful Captain of the group. Within my team, I can recall at least three of the boys who saw themselves as the big kahuna. There was Aris, my best friend, who was so *irritatingly neat*! Fastidious and quick to answer the priest's voice, Aris often got noticed, and was regarded as the most dependable, punctual, and well-organized. Then there was Kosta, who had the voice of an angel, as well as being a hallowed demeanor. From the holy island of Kos, Greece, Kosta was bilingual and had the depth of traditional Orthodox culture. His comportment was flawlessly reverent. He was *irritatingly perfect*! We also had John V., who was *annoyingly efficient*. A bully, he would smack us on the back of the head with his hand that wore a giant ring. Or he would grab our ears and twist them if we did not listen or obey him. John was the guy who got things done and was never to be crossed. Oh, and then there was me. My head seemed to be everywhere, watch-

THE *Fablehood* TRILOGY

ing, and wondering about everything. I was always *frustratingly lost* in the clouds. But I loved the altar, and I knew how to respond with prayer. I knew deep inside where I belonged, and even Father noticed that I was often deep in prayer. My true faith was emerging as I found myself truly moved by the solemnity of the liturgy.

Now, there was a particularly big feast day in the church. I do not recall which day, though it could have during been Holy Week. At any rate, we were together in the *iero*, and a myriad of things needed to be done. There were processions, liturgical movements, folks holding fans, crosses, censers, and at one point, there was a noticeable lull in the action. Nothing "major" was required to be done, no swinging the censer, nor bringing to the altar a loaf of bread or hot water. All that was required was a little faithful attention toward the service, and perhaps a candle for a Gospel entrance but nothing too earth shattering. Father looked over at us all, but not one of us lifted a finger to assist him. He paused and said, "When one of you can stop being so very important, maybe you could help me with the service." Ouch! His words cut me to the core. Were we that shallow and transparent? Were we that full of ourselves? Well, I suppose so. He was one hundred percent correct, and his words humbled me severely. I (we) had it coming. In Greek, we would say, "*Kala na patheis*," meaning, "You deserved such a fate!" The truth was horrible, and I felt so ashamed. We were so into ourselves, so involved in what each of us was doing, so bound up by tunnel vision, that we lost sight of why we were there. We were supposed to be at the holy altar to serve God. Instead, we were only there to serve ourselves. How pathetic!

How easy it is to get caught up in self-importance, even in the Holy of Holies. The sin of pride, or egocentrism, or worship of self, whatever it is called, can oftentimes be difficult to escape, especially when it is bred in subtle tiny steps. The sin of "doxa," self-glorification can be too gentle to detect, until it is too enslaving to unshackle. To wit, I can still hear my mother's words, *"Proseche teen Doxa."* "Be wary of glory!"

CHIP 38: *Never take yourself too seriously. Take your mission seriously. Take God seriously. Take others seriously. Others, with hope, will take you seriously, but leave yourself behind. You will win more support by focusing more on others than on yourself. Never take yourself too seriously.*

39

Bizarre Bazaar Boys

Back then, in the late '60s and early '70s, our beloved Annunciation Church in Lancaster could be found layering trays with phyllo dough, nuts, and honey syrup to make baklava for sale at the annual Greek Bazaar. The parishioners were busy setting the table to offer wonderfully delectable dishes from the Hellenic world to be sold in the American world. The intersection between our sacred community and the outside world passed over a plate of pastitsio, pilafi, and Greek salad, as we became intimate with thousands of our closest famished friends.

The Greek Bazaar is an immense operation that requires the support and buy-in of everyone who considers himself or herself a member of the Annunciation Orthodox Church. Hundreds of hands are needed to cook the various meals, getting them safely in the hands of the public, counting the funds coming in, and ensuring that the right message is communicated from the Church. The whole operation takes months to organize and prepare for the weekend event, usually held in November. The community swelled at this time, and it was not unusual for me, even back then, to see folks, whom I had never seen before, volunteering their time. As much as it was a pleasure to host, the annual bazaar could be downright exhausting. The festival has its bizarre moments as well.

Take my buddies and me, for example, the same boys who volunteered in the holy altar, also stepped up for the Greek Bazaar, or that is what we feigned. We were as dependable as a paper umbrella in a hurricane. The problem was that, while our mothers could be found slaving away at some tables to assemble sumptuous labor-intensive ethnic dishes, we occupied our time in less stressful tasks. We saw ourselves as ambassadors of humor and timely opportunistic, light-hearted distraction, innocent malevolence aimed at releasing some of the steam from the pressure our parents and grandparents were under.

Our official job was to make boxes for takeout items such as pastries and the drive-thru. We did as little as we could with as minimal an effort as was humanly possible. It wasn't that we did not care about the bazaar, but rather that we soon found it all so boring and unentertaining. By virtue of our ennui, coupled with our supposed right to be constantly occupied with pleasure, we took matters into our own hands. And so, after just a few boxes were folded and stacked, we would suddenly drift out, disappearing into the back walls and hallways of the immense church building.

There was, for instance, a set of back stairwells that linked the bell tower to the basement where there was a small kitchen, which during certain evenings was populated by old ladies, who apparently suffered from podiatry issues, as their socks always seemed to be gathered in clumps by their bulky black shoes. These were immigrant Greek women who would spend hours upon hours, stirring syrups, cooking fanciful Greek dishes, assembling pastries, scouring pots and pans, and generally being the backbone apron for the bazaar. They never seemed to get tired nor to flag in their attention to job and detail. An army of old ladies in hair buns and olive-oiled hands would gather in the darkest corners and rooms of the building to do whatever was asked of them. Their only consolation was the company they kept together. In Greek, this sisterly camaraderie is broadly called a *"parea,"* a circle, posse, or set of friends, the group with whom you identify. We would hide in the stairwell and eavesdrop on them, listening intently, to hear them chatting in high-pitched accented tones, in phrases we could not understand in the least. Often, we could hear them singing songs that must have evoked remembrances of the old country. While they were in such reveries, and without the least concern for their privacy, we would search for ways to disturb and annoy them. Our interference was immature and inconsiderate and, of course, terribly disrespectful and inappropriate. Think what you may, but we could not help but get perverse pangs of pleasure, hearing them scream and curse, when we tossed hangers and any loose articles down the stairwell to create a commotion. They must have hated us, as I did recognize one word they used quite often, *"Diavoli"* or devils. We got a kick out of that! But of course, we knew that if we stayed in one place too long, we ran the risk of getting caught or simply getting bored, and so we moved on.

During the actual bazaar itself, my gang of hellions found a wonderful outlet for our creative mayhemic energies. Our job, which we willingly and happily begged the bazaar organizers to allow us to do, was trash duty. We would wait beside each barrel of trash, located at the exits and entrances of the hall, until it reached a point at which it was sufficiently full. Then we would heave out the stuffed bag from inside the barrel, which would require all of us to lift out, tie off the bag, replace it with a new bag, and then haul out the old one to the immense trash bins outside. Then the fun would really begin! After a herculean effort to lift the bag into the increasingly crowded trash bin, we found it necessary to compact the trash further. This we did in a most artful and creative way. We would climb to the top of the giant bin and take turns jumping onto the obese bags below, until we could feel the bottom bags crush and make room for the others. Since this activity was so rough and tumble, it had the unfortunate effect of causing many of the bags to open (not that they were tied off so well to begin with), thus liberating their contents, creating a cauldron of moist unmentionable mixtures, a morass that resulted in an odor so complex, so irredeemably putrid that even a common rodent would have been rightly scandalized. But all those fermenting juices and leftover meals did not intimidate us. We had a job to do! We would not be daunted. After all, the whole event depended upon us.

The next Sunday, and the Sunday after that, and the one after that, and so forth and so on, if you wanted to find us, we could be very easily found. We

THE Fablehood TRILOGY

could be found in the holy altar. (Incidentally, if you looked for those boys today, you would find that two of them are serving as priests).

CHIP 39: *Brotherhood is nurtured in the soils of brotherly play. For even though the foibles of youth may be quite unsightly, and even rude, irritating, and ungainly, they cannot dispel the beauty hidden just below the surface. Even behind the veils and trickeries of immaturity, brothers form in arms and legs and kinks of any kind because the gain of shared experiences outweighs every moral and higher code imaginable. For it matters not if the memories are healthy or poor ones, for whatever draws brothers together keeps them together, even if it is bonded in mudslinging or brick building, or any endeavor or game whatsoever. The shared experiences are what bond brothers together. Brotherhood is nurtured in the soils of brotherly play.*

40

Outside the Sirtaki

I have always been spellbound by the ongoing beauty of Greek dancing. Circling about an imaginary center, dancers would step and flow in prescribed patterns, movements choreographed to forge an image of eternity. On and on in a circle, the bouzouki would strum and pluck in syncopated intervals, lively, spirited, zestful, and aflame with the cycles of birth and death, male and female, potent and decaying, day and night, now and forever. Occasionally, when indicated by the beat, a clarinet would join in with sonorous elegance; it was an ongoing dance, swaying, tilting, lifting, on and on, arm-in-arm, and step-by-step. I spent every summer, and every wedding, and often baptisms, enchanted by the rhythmic flow of Greek dance. I simply watched, enthralled.

But in response, I just sat. I never ventured to clasp hands in the circle myself, although I was always invited. Too self-conscious, too shy, too embarrassed, too left-footed, too much of whatever it was, kept me paralyzed on the outside of the dances. I distinctly recall the terror of attending a church picnic, knowing

THE Fablehood TRILOGY

that as evening came, eight track players would come out, and the dancing would begin under our rented pavilion. I would find myself gazing at the developing affair, the music picking up, and folks joining onto the lines in joyful harmony. I so greatly envied them, yet I would not take a single step forward, or I would pretend to be talking to my friends and family, who themselves would leap into the fray. But again and again, I would not budge. Even when coaxing led to pulling that finally accomplished the goal of joining the circular dance, I would just as soon cut out and find myself on the outside of the pavilion, somewhere safe in the darkness, looking into the warm glow of life within. Even on the occasion when I did jump in, I was overly conscious of the eyes around me, eyes watching my steps, counting and judging them, to remind me when I was going to fail. The sensation of being watched was always something I felt in Greek dancing. I know that because I too was watching others, trying to learn and to fit in. But the eyes transfixed me and left me listless. All this time, I was mesmerized by the music and the movement, but I would not give in to its intoxicating allure. And so, I stepped away.

When I was a child and found myself at one of these dances, I had a perfect antidote to my inability to dance. I found immense joy running in and out between the dancers and whirling between the concentric orbs of their high-stepping shoes. I felt as if I were in an ocean of sound, leaping over the crashing waves, rising and falling with the torrents. As a child, I could manage such an infantile involvement, I suppose because it was perceived as acceptable. But when I was approaching the end of my childhood,

Outside the Sirtaki

and I knew its denouement rather well, I could not settle with such juvenile expressions of dance. Now I had to dance or not to dance. I was desperately wanting to be in the circle, and just as desperately terrified by it. I could not determine what I was supposed to do or who I was meant to be, and had these thoughts about being Greek, being American, being able and athletic, being unable and inadequate. Ugh! All these thoughts and more rushed through my brain, pouring concrete down my torso and legs and finally shackling my feet to the floor. And so, I stood on the outside of the circle, outside the pavilion, outside among the crickets and the fireflies, outside in the cool of the waning summer night, and I was outside as far as I could go. But inside, I wept.

That kind of remorse over Greek dancing would limp in my soul for many years. At one point, I even took lessons, and I got the concepts down rather well, at least intellectually. But whenever I would try to step in a relaxed and rhythmic way, something in my brain would stop me from making much joy in the movement. Oh, I would have the count in my head—nine steps forward and three back—but it was all mechanical, numbers that counted more in my thoughts than in my feet. And so, feeling awkward again, I would feel the eyes all over again.

Now, in my later years, I am less self-conscious, and so when I feel like it, I get up to dance. But alas, my legs do not have the bounce and the coordination in them that they once did. I am not very graceful at all, and it may be a bit late to learn more, perhaps too late, but it is worth every step.

THE Fablehood TRILOGY

CHIP 40: *Just dance! If I have learned anything it is this.... Let go of yourself and just move. Forget how you look, how you appear, what others think, what you can or cannot do. Set yourself free. Let every step exhilarate your senses. Lift off with the pedals God gave you. Just dance!*

41

The Late Great Fear of God

Saint Anthony the Great is reputed to have said, "I no longer fear God, but I love Him." What he alludes to in this quote is not only the power of love, but almost as importantly, the compelling force of fear. Before we can confidently say that we have true affection for the Lord almighty, let alone deep and abiding love for him, we need to ascertain the roots of the relationship. The great desert ascetic describes the spiritual journey required of a faithful supplicant toward God as a movement from the fear of God to bargaining with God, and from bargaining with God to the love of God. Rarely, if ever, does anyone begin their experience of God with love. Fear has always been a more realistic starting point.

It certainly was for me. Without fear, without some sense of imminent threat, I probably would never have changed my attitude toward God. But thanks to the anxiety endemic of the early '70s, there were plenty of opportunities for terror. And, if the era itself was not enough to create anxieties, my dad was more than willing to provide the same.

He was rather busy, obsessed to be more accurate, at reading literature, prophesying the End Times as being just around the corner. Listening to the Reverend Billy Graham, delivering fiery sermons during his crusades, I grew steadily fearful. He spoke so authoritatively, so passionately, so convincingly, that you could be assured that he had some inner connection. He spoke as if he knew for certain what was going to happen in the near future. And so, it seemed wise to listen to someone who had an inside track to the Almighty. Additionally, with the arms race and the Cold War that never seemed to end, there was ample reason to believe that, if we did not find some form of world peace or the Lord soon, and I mean very soon, we were likely to die in an impending nuclear showdown. "Mutually Assured Destruction," or MAD was the insane mantra of the age.

There was also a certain book popular at the time, called *The Late Great Planet Earth*, written by Hal Lindsey, that linked current news items with events described in the Book of Revelation. The author purported that we were "living in the end times," and that the ambiguous prophecies of the Apocalypse were clearly being fulfilled in our current time. Whether the connections were valid, only God could say, but all I knew was that I was increasingly scared to death.

I asked Dad if he truly believed that these ancient prophecies were being manifested in our days or whether he thought we were living at the end of time. Dad not only agreed with Billy Graham and Hal Lindsey, he believed it with all his heart, so much so that Dad repented of his ways and sought to change his life. I was ten years old, and I distinctly recall his dramatic change. He was focused and purposeful, kinder and easier to live with, and he started doing what he never willingly did before—he started attending church regularly. Dad even volunteered to teach Sunday School and to sing in the church choir. He took his role in the church seriously, and actively searched for ways to serve in the community. However, what made his "conversion" experience most impressive, and most convincing to me and others, was that he transferred his natural artistic talents toward the painting of icons, Here, in the arcane world of Byzantine iconography, Dad found his niche and his calling, even though he would tell me, and everybody who would listen, that he felt called to be a priest. Before that ordination ever happened, though, he would make iconography his form of the priesthood. The change in Dad, here, cannot be overstated. It was real and sincere, proven by this commitment to the Lord. Everyone linked to his world could attest to his change in character and behavior. He stopped drinking, he no longer cussed or blew up in rage, he aimed to quit smoking, and, most impressively, he had a new sense of purpose. I am so grateful to God for the religious movements of the mid-70s!

Dad wanted to become an iconographer, something that required study and practice, which he vigorously pursued. He even began a weekly home Bible Study group, to which invited his close circle of friends. I also attended and witnessed how Dad would tell his guests about the Good News that had changed his life. He came to love the Orthodox faith, which he embraced as the true faith—the vehicle that has preserved the message of the Lord unchanged

THE Fablehood TRILOGY

from the beginning. Dad became an ambassador of the Faith that has established the universe. I could not help noticing all of this dramatic change, especially since it was so different from the reality he had exhibited earlier. He was truly a "new man," and I witnessed it without fear or shame. I was deeply grateful and at peace. I believed in his conversion, his change of heart, his complete reversal of self. I believed and I took his life to heart. I, too, have been changed forever by Dad's conversion, both instinctively and with an increasing hunger in my heart. My dad had been "Born Again," and so would I. He was on fire, and so am I.

All of us—Connie, George, and I—were raised to believe in God and received a firm foundation in the faith. The main reason for this solid groundwork was due, I am certain, to my mom's enduring commitment. She was always in church, always volunteering, always helpful to others, always counseling, always listening, always the wisest and sweetest person in any room. She was the model of the Christian woman, and a mother who deeply loved the faith. She was always faithful, and exhibited a devotion that was often stereotypical of women in the church, and women in general—always faithful to the end. This faithfulness only confirmed my mother's abiding commitment.

However, it was only until my father "became a Christian" that I did too. There was something magical, interior, and kinetic about these days while still in my tenth year. Suddenly, a fire arose in my heart, and I knew exactly what I wanted to do with my life. My "Calling" was crystal clear, true in my heart and soul, and plain in seeing the purpose of my life, that had

The Late Great Fear of God

been revealed to me. Yes, I was aided by the great magnifying glass of my father's life, but this calling was mine—a message for me alone—from God. I was certain and had no doubts: I was going to become a priest. And I was going to become a priest for one reason, and one reason alone—it was because the priesthood would give me a fuller voice to express what I believe. I would become a priest to speak immediately, loudly, boldly, and fervently with one simple message: God is with us! I would share this message because it was what I had experienced through my Dad's conversion, and because I, too, was changing as I equipped myself and dedicated myself to this call.

I began spreading the message from my banana seat bike. I would ride my bike down to my football playing friends down in Quaker Hills and share what I had recently learned. Without a doubt or a moment's hesitation, I would declare that the world was coming to an end, and, I would add, rather soon. We could be the target of nuclear destruction any time now. We could be subject to impending natural disaster, societal collapse, and the inexorable unraveling of our society. I declared the truth of this message firmly and with confidence. They would listen gap-jawed and wonder what would happen to them. They were ready, and so I would then share the news with them, the Good News that God has saved us. Most of the boys would listen kindly and attentively, especially when I would invite them to join me in repentance. They were respectful of me and the message I was offering them. Repent and be delivered! The kingdom of heaven is at hand! I knew then that my childhood was over. The priesthood was beginning.

THE Fablehood TRILOGY

CHIP 41: *Discover your moment of epiphany. For each of us, there is a time to discover who we are and our purpose. But first, a little of the child must die before a man can be born; and, a little bit of the child must remain, to know the Lord. Do not eschew fear, for as the psalmist says, "the beginning of wisdom is the fear of God." Fear can also be the launching point of self. Whatever it takes, take it. Discover your moment of epiphany.*

Epilogue

So, after forty-one "chips," I hope the reader is not feeling sick or bloated, since I know how fattening some things can be. Too many chips can be just too many! There comes a time when you have to close the bag and seal it with one of those giant clips. Then, when you have the munchies again, you can grab a few more. For now, it is time to put this bag on the shelf, and hopefully these chips will not go stale.

That, in fact, is probably why I wrote this gastronomically themed work, so that the chips would not wilt or spoil or lose their flavor. On the contrary, I wanted you to taste them just as I have, and with hope that you have found them as delicious as I have. Truth be told, I am still hankering for these chips, so I'll write another bag—stuffed with crisps from my teenage years.

In the meantime, as you digest these, I am certain that you have gathered that I am not simply dealing in snacks, but rather with the experiences that are the cuisine of my life. My intention in writing this little volume was to give you a sense of who I am, and why I am this way. I pray that I have succeeded, and I am hoping that you, my beloved reader, my children

THE Fablehood TRILOGY

and grandchildren, and anyone else who has a weakness for chips, will be able to sift out the extra salt and vinegar that may have been sprinkled here and there. A little seasoning is a good thing to make the soul wink and wince occasionally. I hope that some of the salt found the corners of your eyes. Indeed, I would be delighted if you sometimes laughed and sometimes paused in reflection. I hope you enjoyed these chips and are in the mood for more.

By the way, in reading these little vignettes, if you found that my mind's eye, memory, or even credibility may have seemed a little suspect at times, please forgive me. To the best of my knowledge, each and every one of these stories is historically accurate and true.

But it is my heartfelt hope that these personal stories have touched you in a positive and edifying way. Quite obviously, I wanted to touch you with the story of my life, so that I could offer you what I know about the world you came from, and so that you may discover yourself in the world you inhabit. From my heart to yours....

This set of stories is my gift to you.

A COLUMN OF CHIPS

Having grown up in the snack mecca of the universe, also known as Central Pennsylvania, I can certainly attest that Utz chips are the best around. Well, at least that's my salt on the topic. But I would be remiss if I were not to recognize the genius behind the "Pringle" stack. Pressed into uniform ranks, as if designed by Prussian officers. These sculpted saltine

Epilogue

scallops settle neatly into shingled stacks. They form enticing sleeves for the *nosher* to disrupt with ravenous hands.

My own "Column of Chips," however, are not so artfully arranged, not even close. Like life itself, they are uneven, odd fitting, and vary in intensity. They are not uniform in the least. They just are, just like each of us. I offer them here in their entirety for the reader to peruse and snack at his or her leisure. Enjoy the salt!

• ✳ •

CHIP 1: *Never force; always encourage. In my life, I have rarely, if ever, responded well to motivation by force or coercion. I simply learned to dig in my heels from two years old. Consequently, I have rarely, if ever, motivated others, especially my own children, by compulsion, pressure, or force. Never force; always encourage.*

CHIP 2: Beauty is an eternal inspiration. In my life, I have always been blessed by what is beautiful and artful, and I thank my father for that gift. Hence, for me, everything I do, say, or think is measured by whether it is well-composed and beautiful. The on-going search for beauty captivates me and is my inspiration toward the eternal. Beauty is an eternal inspiration.

CHIP 3: *Never forget to say thanks. Some gifts in life can never actually be repaid. At such times, and with such folks, all you can do is say, "Thank you." This remembrance to be grateful is a graceful attitude of the heart, one that brings good perspective to the movement of life. In all things, both seen and unseen, Never forget to say thanks.*

THE Fablehood TRILOGY

CHIP 4: *Imagination is the glider of the mind. A person is never truly alone, even when he is alone. Sometimes, perhaps most of the time, our best company is our own imagination. Our thoughts and our dreams can take us to incredible realms. With our imagination, we are never by ourselves. Imagination is the glider of the mind.*

CHIP 5: *Love has powerful arms. Love carries us, always, even when we are unaware or completely blind of its immense power. No matter our age or situation, no matter how strong or independent we may feel, no matter what our conditions may be, we all need and hunger for love, affection, and attention. And sometimes, by the grace of God, we receive it, even when we do not know it is there, but once known, it is never forgotten. Love has powerful arms.*

CHIP 6: *Listen twice; advance once. Listen carefully to the words of someone who has gone before you. They are wise for a reason. God provides each of us with advocates and advisors all along the way of life. Heed them. Listen twice; advance once.*

CHIP 7: *Truth always prevails. And this is so because truth is far stronger than fear. Even though fear can intimidate, paralyze, and devastate one's forward journey. Unopposed, evil wins. But the proclamation of truth, conveyed by courage, never fails. Where truth is insisted upon, lovingly, gently, inexorably, it always triumphs. Truth always prevails.*

CHIP 8: *Never judge a lemon by its peel. There is more pulp to the fruit than meets the eyes. So it is with people; and so, never judge a sourpuss by the sour. Maybe they just want to be noticed and appreciated. A little love goes a long way to sweetening the sour. Never judge a lemon by its peel.*

Epilogue

CHIP 9: Each of us has our own distinctive fingerprint. No two are ever alike. God has a blessing for each of us, and each of us is called to give back that blessing to God. This act of returning the gift to the Great Giver is the stuff of life and the incense of God's glorification. There is no jealousy or strife, then, when we recall that every one of us is one-of-a-kind and once-for-all-time. We are all designed to fulfill life with our gifts and give God the glory. Each of us has our own distinctive fingerprint.

CHIP 10: The tongue is the rudder of Love. How it moves changes the world one syllable and breath at a time. When it is withheld or misdirected, it wounds. But when properly steered the tongue directs the journey of life. A word well-intended can change the navigator's arc. So it is that Love, on any level, creates its own language. This common language, even between rival brothers, keeps us together, even when we are pulling apart. The tongue is the rudder of Love.

CHIP 11: A falling star never fails; it always inspires even in its descent. Occasionally, God sends us a shooting star, if for no other reason than to renew our belief in the heavens and in the wonder of it all. Uncle Tom may your memory be eternal. A falling star never fails; it always inspires even in its descent.

CHIP 12: Less is more. If a Christmas tree needs pruning and benefits from trimming, then the same applies to persons. A little personal editing is a good, and necessary, thing. Less is more.

CHIP 13: No blue is bluer than the holiday blue. There is no surprise that "The Holidays" exacerbate tender wounds and brittle relationships, especially because folks are gathered so close together. In such circumstances, after the wounding, one can forgive an injury, and one must, but the debilitation in one's soul may last for years and

THE Fablehood TRILOGY

years. There is a reason for the shades and hues. No blue is bluer than the holiday blue.

CHIP 14: An odd-shaped gem still casts a radiant glint. Love knows no borders or restraints but joins according to its one will, wherever and however and to whomever it wills. Love governs itself and hews to no one. Love is universal and invincible and ever beautiful, no matter who the subject may be. An odd-shaped gem still casts a radiant glint.

CHIP 15: Family tables are full of all kinds of fruits and nuts. We cannot help if they are our loved ones and relatives. Pass the gravy and move on. And, to keep the peace, unless asked, keep your opinions to yourself. Family tables are full of all kinds of fruits and nuts.

CHIP 16: Gain and pain are rooted in the nearness of love. This is especially true when one is discovering themselves, for nothing is so disquieting, nay, disruptive than the emergence of the Self. The surprise traits, the personal blemish that cannot be powdered over, the knowledge that you are somehow different, that you are in society but do not have a place there—these are all hidden pains of emerging as a unique person. So it is, then, that childhood innocence cannot bear the terrifying aspects of maturity, especially when it must shoulder the heartbreaking of private suffering. Gain and pain are rooted in the nearness of love.

CHIP 17: A small slice is preferable to an entire pie. Brief and frequent is better than occasional and drawn out. To wit, we benefit most when we can see one another more often, with short visits, with bursts of flavor, rather than rarely and gorging for a long time. A small slice is preferable to an entire pie.

CHIP 18: *"Pan metron ariston."* Everything in moderation. The middle way is often the wisest. But the extremes are rather attractive as well! The middle of the road is the

Epilogue

best part to travel on. But the far sides provide adventures of their own. But for the sake of sanity and clarity, stick to the heart of the road. *"Pan metron ariston."* Everything in moderation.

CHIP 19: No cry can ever be completely muffled. There is a suffering that does not involve blood or violence, but rather, sobs quietly and silently beneath the surface of the skin. And, sadly, there is no cosmetic that can cover it completely. The soul will find its cavern in which to wail, no matter what. No cry can ever be completely muffled.

CHIP 20: Blood can be enriched by water. Blood relatives do not have to remain relatives. They can even be people you admire, people you want in your life, people with whom you choose to associate; relatives can even become friends. Blood can mix with water and be neither diluted nor saturated. Indeed, blood can be enriched by water.

CHIP 21: A comet is never encountered without a gaping mouth. Some folks are comets. An impression does not have to take long to be truly impressive; It is the depth that matters, not the length. Like the sudden appearance of a deer in a yard or a dolphin from the beach, a shooting star, or even a soaring comet, can affect a person more in a moment than in a lifetime of starry nights. A comet is never encountered without a gaping mouth.

CHIP 22: Gild the passing of time. For a moment once lived will never come again, even one shared by billions of siblings. This is because eternity only occurs in the present. Gild the passing of time.

CHIP 23: Every mold is cast once. No one is cast in a single shape. We are all as complex and beautifully crafted as any of Michelangelo's sculptures. We each have rough hews and smooth polishes. Each sculpture is lovely and unique. Every mold is cast once.

THE Fablehood TRILOGY

CHIP 24: A snail without a shell is just a slug. We all need a place, a niche to live in. Every man craves his own castle, even if he must hang a barber pole out front to claim it. Likewise, every man needs to declare his own style, even if it means turning his back on the old and familiar. We crave to be ourselves. A snail without a shell is just a slug.

CHIP 25: We all have a place at the table, our own special chair. The royal ones earn their thrones, and all the ladies and gentlemen in waiting benefit from their largesse. For not all of us sit at the head of the table. Some are more regal than others but make everyone feel at ease where they sit. But we all sit together. We all have a place at the table, our own special chair.

CHIP 26: The side road is the compelling one. Be sure to take an occasional road trip to nowhere. On your return, you will find that you have been to somewhere memorable and renewing. Take a trip and do not be afraid. It is the drive that matters. Or, to quote the inimitable poet, Mr. Frost, "Take the road less taken." The side road is the compelling one.

CHIP 27: Never leave your vacation, even if you must go home. The world, with all its wonder and beauty, is discovered with one unnecessary adventure at a time, and blissfully recalled one memory at a time. Your mind is an enduring Coney Island. Never leave your vacation, even if you must go home.

CHIP 28: Healing begins and goes on with the Healer's touch. Good health is a balance of the forces in one's life, and we are blessed when we have someone to help us keep this balance. We are assured by the wisdom of those who have gone before us. It is thus wise to heed what they say and advise. To be healthy, then, follow the healthy. Be ready to perceive when you are touched. Healing begins and goes on with the Healer's touch.

Epilogue

CHIP 29: Learning craves a moment. Never lose an opportunity to reach someone with a teachable moment. If necessary, use alternative methods, but do whatever it takes to reach them and teach them. Never, ever give up on anyone, especially where learning is concerned! Find the time, find the way, and find the key. Learning craves a moment.

CHIP 30: A word of kindness never fails. Class begets class, and barbarism begets barbarism. We become who we model. Or, quite simply, "The apple does not fall too far from the tree." I have been blessed to benefit from good people, folks who lifted me up by their simple civility, a disposition not accidental but learned in the home and shared abroad. Thank God for such social smoothing. My life has been the better for simple words and actions. A word of kindness never fails.

CHIP 31: All DNAs are not created equal. Thankfully, we are all different. There is always someone who is going to be better than you are and someone who is worse than you are. That is okay. We are all designed by a Divine Artist. Accept who you are. All DNAs are not created equal. Thankfully, we are all different.

CHIP 32: There is nothing random about the "people along the way." Think of all the "bus stops" in life, where you get to meet folks who fill up your time with color and commentary. They are gifts from God for a passing time, and then you move on. God puts individuals in our lives to enlarge us and to benefit others. For kindness among so-called "strangers" is heavenly hospitality. So, seize the moments, and the personalities in them, while you can. Life is full of people of joy, even in their sadness, if only we would wake up and respond to them. Embrace the bus stops. Just remember: There is nothing random about the "people along the way."

THE Fablehood TRILOGY

CHIP 33: Love, once experienced, never dies. Even if the exchange of affection happened in early springs of youth or in autumnal or wintry climes, Love endures and is eternal. We are formed by gestures of love, sustained in their ability to lift us out of the moment and into eternal remembrance. The heart is a muscle that never forgets, especially when it has received gifts from another. Love, once experienced, never dies.

CHIP 34: Childhood is a necessary playground for life. We are blessed when we have ample time and freedom to play; we are hindered and hampered when we don't. For a healthy maturity is forged in pretend land and wounded by too much reality. Thank God when we are blessed with backyards of friendship, places simply to be and to let go, where adventures are just a spin or two away, and there is immeasurable time to imagine. Childhood is a necessary playground for life.

CHIP 35: Act your best at each stage in life. It has been said by a certain famous bard that "all of life's a stage," lived one act at a time. Truer words could not have been said, for whatever the stage we are upon in our personal theater, we would be wise to follow some good advice—and that is to be the very height of ourselves each time. Life is a revolving stage, and we are given a cameo role upon cameo role, testing us, challenging us, imploring us to be the utmost that we can be. Regret is not an illusion; it is itself regrettable. Therefore, let us choose wisely whenever we can. Act your best at each stage in life.

CHIP 36: An opportunity lost is a regret forever. Thus, it is wise to avoid climbing trees when a revving auto is available to take you further along in your journey. In fact, you may gain knowledge or a valuable lifelong skill by welcoming the opportunity when it is granted to you. The truth is that a door does not stay open forever, and once closed, is difficult to open again. Walk through the

Epilogue

door of learning while it is offered or suffer its woeful closure. An opportunity lost is a regret forever.

CHIP 37: Never pretend to be someone you are not. There is no shortage of pressures in life to please others, particularly when trying to satisfy those who share your genetic code. These folks who orbit our lives certainly mean well, but their intentions can unintentionally become traps and snares, where one can easily lose an irreplaceable paw. The truth is that our pawprints are ours and ours alone. And so, do be most grateful for loving counsel, but be wary of it when it blurs your own footprint. Fight ferociously to take your own steps in life. Never pretend to be someone you are not.

CHIP 38: Never take yourself too seriously. Take your mission seriously. Take God seriously. Take others seriously. Others, with hope, will take you seriously, but leave yourself behind. You will win more support by focusing more on others than on yourself. Never take yourself too seriously.

CHIP 39: Brotherhood is nurtured in the soils of brotherly play. For even though the foibles of youth may be quite unsightly, and even rude, irritating, and ungainly, they cannot dispel the beauty hidden just below the surface. Even behind the veils and trickeries of immaturity, brothers form in arms and legs and kinks of any kind because the gain of shared experiences outweighs every moral and higher code imaginable. For it matters not if the memories are healthy or poor ones, for whatever draws brothers together keeps them together, even if it is bonded in mudslinging or brick building, or any endeavor or game whatsoever. The shared experiences are what bond brothers together. Brotherhood is nurtured in the soils of brotherly play.

CHIP 40: Just dance! If I have learned anything it is this.... Let go of yourself and just move. Forget how you look,

THE Fablehood TRILOGY

how you appear, what others think, what you can or cannot do. Set yourself free. Let every step exhilarate your senses. Lift off with the pedals God gave you. Just dance!

CHIP 41: Discover your moment of epiphany. For each of us, there is a time to discover who we are and our purpose. But first, a little of the child must die before a man can be born; and, a little bit of the child must remain, to know the Lord. Do not eschew fear, for as the psalmist says, "the beginning of wisdom is the fear of God." Fear can also be the launching point of self. Whatever it takes, take it. Discover your moment of epiphany.

Made in the USA
Middletown, DE
17 March 2023

26955999R00125